THE REMEDY

THE REMEDY

BRINGING
LEAN THINKING
out of **THE FACTORY** *to*
TRANSFORM THE
ENTIRE ORGANIZATION

PASCAL
DENNIS

WILEY

John Wiley & Sons, Inc.

Published by John Wiley & Sons, Inc., Hoboken, New Jersey.
Published simultaneously in Canada.

For general information on our other products and services or for technical support, please contact our Customer Care Department within the United States at (800) 762-2974, outside the United States at (317) 572-3993 or fax (317) 572-4002.

Wiley also publishes its books in a variety of electronic formats. Some content that appears in print may not be available in electronic books. For more information about Wiley products, visit our web site at www.wiley.com.

Library of Congress Cataloging-in-Publication Data:

Dennis, Pascal, 1957–
   The remedy : bringing lean thinking out of the factory to transform the entire organization/Pascal Dennis.
      p. cm.
   Includes index.
   ISBN 978-0-470-55685-6 (cloth)
   1.   Organizational effectiveness.   2.   Total quality management.   I. Title.
   HD58.9.D46 2010
   658.4'013—dc22

                                                                          2010003435

Printed in the United States of America

10 9 8 7 6 5 4 3 2 1

In memory of Katherine Guselle (1935–2008),
artist, activist, mother, and grandmother.
We miss you, Kathy. Hope you're up
there giving Bob a hard time.

Contents

Acknowledgments

I'm grateful to all the good people who have helped to make this book a reality, and I acknowledge them here.

Richard Narramore, Senior Editor, for his light touch and big picture perspective. Lauren Freestone for her deft editing. Lydia Dimitriadis and the Wiley team for their seamless support.

The Lean Pathways team with whom it is my privilege to work. *Open mind, teamwork, challenge!*

All my senseis over the years. (You know who you are.) I hope you will overlook this book's many shortcomings.

Our friends and colleagues at client companies. Thanks for your openness, tenacity, and skill.

Dianne Caton, artist extraordinaire, who has made magic out of my chicken scratch.

Special thanks to Alistair Norval, my colleague, mentor, and friend— who has taught me more than I can say. *This could work indeed . . .*

And finally, my dear wife, Pamela, and our children, Eleanor, Katie, and Matthew.

About the Author

Pascal Dennis is a professional engineer, author, and advisor to international organizations making the Lean leap. Pascal developed his skills by working with major international companies including Toyota in North America and Japan.

Pascal is a multiple winner of the Shingo Prize and the author of *Lean Production Simplified: A Plain Language Guide to the World's Most Powerful Production System*; the business novel, *Andy & Me*; and *Getting the Right Things Done: A Leader's Guide to Planning and Execution*.

Pascal lives in Toronto with his wife and three children.

For more information please visit www.leanpathwaysinc.com.

Preface

Why a book about Lean *outside* the factory?

Because that's where the opportunity lies. *Upstream*—in marketing, design, and engineering. *Downstream*—in distribution, sales, and customer service. These, together with health care, service, and government, are Lean's frontier. I am less and less a factory rat.

Every core Lean principle applies outside the factory. But business processes are harder to fix.

Why a sequel to *Andy & Me?*

The characters of Tom Papas and Andy Saito seemed a natural vehicle. Readers seem to like them, and I do too.

We're emerging from an economic catastrophe, which claimed many great companies and put millions of people out of work. Lean has the potential to reduce human misery and increase human happiness by doing more with less, while providing meaningful work.

That's enough for me.

Chapter 1 Motor City Sadness

The Boeing 737 rose above the LaGuardia Airport tarmac. Across the East River was Manhattan's symphonic skyline. Below me, Queens was spread out like an abstract expressionist painting, something Jackson Pollock might have produced after a bad hangover. My girl-friend, Sarah, is rubbing off on me. She loves art and literature. When she isn't teaching kindergarten in Hoboken, she is guiding me through the Metropolitan, Guggenheim, and Frick galleries, and through the experimental art galleries that flourish in Brooklyn's nooks and crannies.

I don't mind at all. As an engineering student, my electives were usually art, literature, or psychology. My pals looked at me cockeyed but all that learning served me well when I became an auto plant manager.

Tom Papas is my name. Our family name is Papachristodoulou. My brother Harry and I shortened it, we said, to fit on the back of our football jerseys. Harry is a PhD biochemist, a big wheel in pharmaceuticals, where you can charge 80 bucks for a little pill. I'm plant manager of New Jersey Motor Manufacturing (NJMM), which is part of Taylor Motors. We transform substandard processes, a spaghetti-like supply chain, and rigid management system into the Desperado, a magical muscle car the public loves. What do we get for our efforts? Negative margins and a catastrophic balance sheet. But I don't have to tell you how Taylor Motors is doing. You've heard it all.

Rachel Armstrong, our formidable senior vice president, has summoned me to headquarters in Taylor City, a Motown suburb synonymous with our company. Would she offer me the job of Vice-President of Continuous Improvement again? I turned it down once before because of all the travel required—too hard on my children.

NJMM, and manufacturing in general, is one of Taylor Motors' few bright spots. During the past five years I've become the toast of the company, the superhero credited with resurrecting the NJMM plant, and regaining some luster for our brand. Superhero thinking is a problem for us. If something good happens, we assume heroism—as if the normal functioning of our management system is incapable of producing great results.

At NJMM we make our production numbers every day—with minimal overtime. Our quality is the best in the Taylor system, and world-class in our segment. (Still way behind Lexus, though.) The new Desperado sports car has been a hit and the brand has regained its mystique. Sales, however, are down 25 percent since the economy collapsed—better than most car brands. I've been able to keep all our people employed. But I fear that J. Ed Morgan, our nefarious CFO, may try to chop a shift.

When our plant was facing extinction five years ago, I told my team that we were going "back to school" to learn "Lean," the business system Toyota made famous, and that's been deepened and extended by the world's best companies

Our team members took it to heart, taking Lean books home with them, reading, reflecting, and practicing what they'd read. People are still learning. Not just managers, but also team leaders and team members. I made a deal with them. *You do everything I ask of you, and I promise nobody will lose his or her job because of improvement work.*

Since then, members of the NJMM team have become teachers through our on-site Lean Learning Centre. We've now put more than 200 senior managers, engineers, and team leaders through our "boot camps." As a result, there's a growing network of Lean learners in our manufacturing division. Losing a shift, if that's what Ed Morgan is planning, would be a terrible blow to NJMM morale, and would make a liar out of me.

The jet settled into its cruising altitude and the flight attendant offered us refreshments. It was a fine spring day. I had some water with ice and looked out the window at feathery clouds and a bright blue sky. I thought about how I got here.

We've been lucky at NJMM. Our *sensei*[1] is Takinori (Andy) Saito, an ex-Toyota heavyweight I coaxed out of retirement.[2] Andy has played Virgil to my Dante, leading us out of a manufacturing inferno. Every door that Andy opens leads to three other doors. At times I feel we're more screwed up than ever. Problems are painfully obvious, root causes elusive, and countermeasures—real countermeasures, not Band-Aids—rare. Yet we're winning quality and productivity awards! I always feel, "How could they give us an award? We have so many problems . . . ."

Socrates expressed it well: *The more I know, the more I realize I don't know.* Andy laughed when I told him. "Tom-san, I have been practicing for 40 years—and I still feel like a beginner!"

Toyota's recent fall from grace clearly pained Andy and reinforced how difficult it was to sustain Lean excellence. "To support growth, we must grow senseis, Tom-san . . ."

Andy was encouraged that Toyota had applied its core principle—Stop production, don't ship junk—while they sought root causes. He was heartened that Toyota had accepted responsibility and not thrown their supplier under the bus. There was much reflection in Toyoda City, he told me. Hansei, the Japanese call it; the sincere acknowledgement of mistakes and weakness, and the commitment to improve.

I had a number of chats with my pal Dean Formica, who was Paint Shop General Manager at Toyota's Kentucky plant.

---

[1] Japanese for teacher, mentor, or "one who has gone before."
[2] Readers interested in the rest of the story are referred to *Andy & Me: Crisis and Transformation on the Lean Journey,* by yours truly.

It was an emotional topic for him. "Lots of soul-searching around here, Tommy. We've had two tough years in a row, after 60 good ones."

"What's the root cause, Dino?"

"I agree with Saito-san. We've grown faster than our ability to develop senseis. Our system is a way of thinking and being. You can't absorb it overnight. You need to study for years under the guidance of a capable teacher."

"You certainly have lost senseis," I commented. "People like me have benefited. Working with Andy has changed my life."

"We miss him," Dean said.

I felt a twinge of guilt. "I can imagine . . . So what's next?"

"We're going to bear down and relearn our system. Toyota University is up and running. I've signed up to be an instructor. We're going to do everything we can to regain our customers' trust. I love this company . . ."

Andy taught me to draw things out, to express ideas and learning points with simple sketches. My journals are full of them. Figure 1.1 shows my factory doodle.

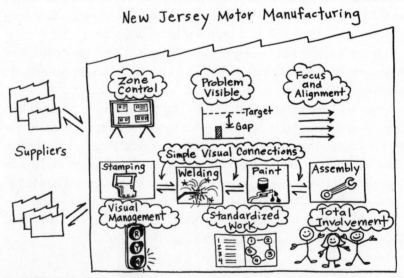

Copyright © 2010 by Lean Pathways Inc.

FIGURE 1.1   New Jersey Motor Manufacturing

We've tried to connect our processes—Stamping, Welding, Paint, and Assembly—with simple visual management. That means using kanbans—simple signals that tell suppliers what to make. In Stamping, kanbans are triangular pieces of metal that tell operators *what* to make, how *many*, and *where* to deliver it. In my dad's restaurant, kanbans are the chits that waiters and waitresses push through the serving window. In your car, the gas gauge acts as a kanban, telling you when it's time to fill up.

For us, *customer* means anyone in our downstream process, and *supplier* means anyone in the upstream process. Suppliers in our plant provide the volume, mix, and sequence that the customer consumes. But here's the catch, they supply only at the required rate and quality level, no more, no less. "Simple handshakes," we call it. We also try to make problems noticeable and involve all team members in their solutions, rather than trying to pin the blame on individuals. Pretty simple, really.

Andy taught us that a problem is simply a *deviation from a standard*, and that problems were *treasures*. Problems tell us how we can improve. Each year we try to focus our improvement work through strategy deployment or *hoshin kanri*, the world's most powerful planning and execution system.[3] We found strategy deployment tough the first few years but are getting the hang of it. In a nutshell, it involves:

- Defining True North, your strategic and philosophical objective.
- Identifying the obstacles preventing you from achieving True North.
- Engaging everybody in the company in the solution.
- Applying and sharing what you've learned.

Again, pretty simple—but hard to do. I've learned that complexity is a crude state. Simplicity marks the end of a process of refining.

Our factory is a part of a vast management system that includes marketing, design, engineering, the supply chain, and our dealer network, not to mention all our business processes, including Finance,

---

[3] For more information on strategy deployment, the reader is referred to *Getting the Right Things Done—Leader's Guide to Planning and Execution* (Cambridge, MA: LEI Publications, 2006).

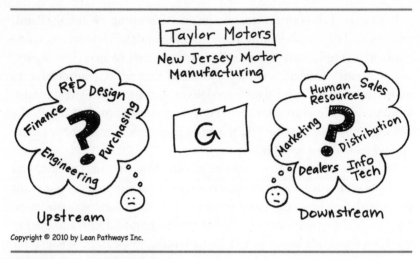

FIGURE 1.2 Taylor Motors

Purchasing, Information Technology, Human Resources, and Planning and Scheduling. We have 10 global design centers and 8 global engineering centers. Our supply chain comprises hundreds of Tier 1, 2, and 3 suppliers in a spaghetti-like distribution system.

See my Taylor Motors sketch in Figure 1.2.

So how do we get out of our current mess? Fixing our factories is necessary—but not sufficient. In my view, manufacturing is no longer the constraint. The remedy lies in dispersing the thick *fog* that envelops our entire company. By fog I mean the lack of transparency and communication, the absence of simple, understandable processes, and simple handshakes between suppliers and customers. I mean the lack of clarity around business objectives, and the lack of focus and alignment on the means of achieving them. I mean not knowing whether you're ahead or behind, whether you're winning or losing the game, because you lack clear scoreboards and simple feedback loops. I also mean the fog of complexity that we mistake for profundity, so we keep quiet during interminable meetings and let the PowerPoint junk run on.

I can't see downstream of our factory—can't see customer demand or how much inventory we and our dealers are carrying. Planning changes our production schedule each week. When I press our planners, it's clear that they don't really know what models, colors, and options are selling. The constant churning creates havoc in our factory, and for our suppliers, who never know what to expect.

Upstream is equally murky. I don't *really* know what the customer likes or dislikes about the Desperado or where we stand compared to the competition. I don't know why our manufacturing equipment and processes are designed the way they are. I don't know what marketing campaigns are in the pipeline or what these campaigns are trying to achieve. I don't know our dealers' incentive structures or why they promote one model over another.

After hearing me describe the fog, Sarah read me a poem by Matthew Arnold. Here are the last few lines:

> And we are here as on a darkling plain
> Swept with confused alarms of struggle and flight,
> Where ignorant armies clash by night.

"Bingo!" I said.

Sarah laughed out loud. "You have a way with words, Tom."

Like surfing, soccer, or ice hockey, manufacturing is about *flow*—flow of information, material, and people. My gut tells me that design, engineering, marketing, and the rest are also about flow—flow of *knowledge*. But beyond here all I have is questions.

What does knowledge flow look and feel like? Do people who work in business functions *think* differently? If so, what are the main differences and how do we accommodate them? What other obstacles do we face? How do we get around them?

Waste is waste. The customer doesn't care whether the launch was delayed by the factory, or by some upstream process. Her bottom line is, "Where's my vehicle?"

At NJMM we've started to apply Lean basics in finance, purchasing, planning, and other administrative areas—with mixed results. Team members in administrative roles seem uncomfortable with visual management, standardization, and continuous improvement. They seem to be afraid to make problems visible. Do they believe it reflects badly on them? Do they fear standardized work will turn them into robots? When I tell them problems are treasures, or that standards are simply a foundation for improvement—they look at me funny.

I winced at the scale of the problem. "You are grasping the situation, Tom-san," Andy told me.

Andy is more than my sensei—he's my friend. When we met, I was in bad shape. Our factory was about to close down, and I was coming out of a terrible divorce with a vindictive ex-spouse. She wouldn't let me see my little girls and seemed to enjoy tormenting me. When I told Andy about it at the Iron Horse, our regular watering hole, he smiled sadly. "Some problems have no countermeasure, Tom-san. One day they just go away."

I didn't know that Andy had resigned Toyota in despair and guilt over the loss of his wife, Shizuko. She had died a difficult death from cancer. But for a long time she had concealed her illness from Andy. He was launching a breakthrough vehicle for Toyota and was on his way to becoming President of Toyota North America.

"She was my wife, my best friend, my biggest supporter," Andy had told me. "But when she needed me I was not there."

I once asked Andy what he believed in. "Open mind, teamwork, challenge," he replied. "Now I add one more—*family*. But too late . . ."

I remember learning the cardinal virtues at St. Irene's Sunday school in Astoria: Temperance, Prudence, Courage, and Justice.[4] For a long time, they were just abstractions. But my sensei paid a terrible price for his ambition, for his lack of *temperance*. Would I make the same mistake? I knew I was prone to it.

Andy's loneliness also worries me. He spends his winters in Kyushu, near his daughters Yumi and Yamiko. But the rest of the year he's alone in his house in Essex Fells, working on his garden. I was hoping Andy would meet a nice lady at the Japanese Cultural Centre in Jersey City, where he took meditation class. I met Yumi and Yamiko last year. "You are a great friend to papa-san," they told me. "He is my friend and sensei," I replied. "I would do anything for him."

Things are somewhat better with my ex-wife, Teal Orcutt. She was born into one of New Jersey's oldest families, a debutante, the whole

---

[4] For more on the cardinal virtues, the interested reader is directed to *A Short Treatise on the Great Virtues*, by Andre Comte-Sponville (New York: Henry Holt, 1996).

thing. She writes a society column and blog for a major media conglomerate. Our children, Helen and Sophie, are 12 and 10. To get regular time with them, I took Teal to court—and won, or so I thought. Teal played ball and was even nice to me for a while—until I got serious about Sarah. Since then we've had some rocky moments. I'm tired of it. I want peace with the mother of my children. We've suffered enough.

The flight attendant refilled my plastic cup with water. This morning, before driving to LaGuardia Airport, I stopped for breakfast at the Humpty Dumpty Bar & Grill, my parents' Greek town restaurant in Astoria, Queens. It's a joint at the corner of 31st Street and Ditmars Boulevard. There's a neon sign out front—Humpty taking a header, which for a long time seemed a metaphor for my life.

I'd had an early morning workout and was hungry. After greeting my parents, Nick and Noula, Uncle Louie, and the rest of the crew, I ordered the Corfu special—three eggs lightly whipped with a dash of cream, ham, olives, tomatoes, green pepper, and feta cheese, and a tomato salad. Mama's famous spanakopita, a spinach and feta cheese pie that melted in your mouth, rounded out the meal.

When the breakfast rush was over, my parents joined me for Greek coffee. Mama was beaming about Sarah. "Such a nice girl, Tommy, after all you went through. Each night I thank St. Spyridon for your good fortune. God bless you, chriso mou."

St. Spyridon is the patron saint of Corfu, the beautiful island where my parents were born. I'm hoping to take Sarah and the girls there next summer.

Dad was full of beans, as usual.

"TOM PAPAS—*PAPACHRISTODOULOU*, I SHOULD SAY. MY SON! LOOK AT HIM, NOULA. PLANT MANAGER! BIG SHOT! REMEMBER WHEN HE AND HIS BROTHER WERE SQUIRTS RUNNING AROUND THE RESTAURANT? HOW THE YEARS FLY BY . . ."

He has a howitzer-voice, big nose, and a grin full of gold teeth. Remember John Belushi in the old *Saturday Night Live* routine? That's my dad. *Cheeseborg, Cheeseborg, Cheeseborg . . . No Coke—Pepsi!*

"Not so loud, Nicky," said Mama, "the customers are looking at you."

"OF COURSE THEY ARE LOOKING! AND WHAT DO THEY SEE? A PROUD FATHER—THAT'S ME! AND HIS SON, THAT'S TOMMY!"

Mama made a mock appeal to heaven. "What are we going to do with him, Tommy?"

But I know she's concerned about Dad's health. Heart trouble runs on Dad's side of the family and he has all the symptoms: fatigue, sleeplessness, loss of appetite. Luckily, Harry and I have inherited Mama's robust health. My parents have worked pedal to the metal for 40 years. They've always seemed indomitable, the rock on which Harry and I have built our lives. It's hard for me to imagine them slowing down.

We finally persuaded Dad to see a doctor. Every month we take him to Mount Sinai hospital for check-ups. I can't help noticing all the waste there:

- Delay waste everywhere—*patient* is the right term.
- Overprocessing waste in the multiple handoffs between specialties.
- Conveyance waste in having to troop around from clinic to clinic.
- Rework waste caused by errors in diagnosis, and God forbid, treatment.
- Motion waste in all the workers I see running around looking for things.
- Inventory waste in all the patients waiting for something to happen in the vast warehouse they call a hospital.
- Knowledge waste in all these smart, dedicated people working in obviously broken processes.

The absence of visual management and standardized work is also painfully obvious. I ask hospital workers basic questions, like:

- How is each patient doing?
- What are the biggest risks each patient is facing?
- Who is the case leader?
- What's today's workload?
- Are you ahead or behind?

I know I'm a pain—I can't help it. My questions elicit either blank stares or assurances that, "It's in the computer." That's what we used to say at NJMM. We've learned that "what's in the computer" is usually *wrong*.

"I don't trust this place," I told Harry. "The people seem okay, but the processes are hopeless."

Harry knows the system. "Your instincts are right," he said. "The system is made up of deep, deep silos. Everybody specializes. But the connections *between* silos are informal, so handoffs are bad. Nobody can see the big picture. Patients fall through the cracks."

I'm not surprised by the epidemic of hospital-induced or "nosocomial" deaths—caused by infections, wrong medication, wrong dose, and the like. In hospitals, I see the same fog that afflicts Taylor Motors. I'm worried that my dad might become another statistic.

Working at the Humpty Dumpty as a kid, I learned the nitty-gritty of running a business. I learned about value, waste, flow, pull, and other core Lean concepts.[5] I also met wonderful characters. My parents didn't call it Lean, of course. It was just common sense. Figure 1.3 shows the "Waste Wheel" I drew out when Andy began working with us.

Andy defined value as *what the customer is willing to pay for*. Everything else is waste, or *muda* in Japanese. At the Humpty Dumpty I experienced each form of waste viscerally. Motion waste, for example, means sore feet. The best waiters and waitresses effortlessly serve multiple tables with minimal motion. They always add value whenever they move—by greeting a customer, clearing a table, or closing out a tab.

Waiting waste means unhappy customers who don't come back. Conveyance waste means unnecessary trips to the farmer's market to get our meat and produce. Correction or scrap waste means making the wrong thing, or overcooking something, and having to throw it out. Overprocessing means too many steps in a process, so you fall behind—a killer during the breakfast and lunch rush. Inventory waste means carrying more raw materials than you need, which means either throwing stuff out when it goes bad, or buying a bigger fridge.

---

[5] For a detailed discussion of these and other core Lean concepts, please refer to *Lean Production Simplified—A Plain Language Guide to the World's Most Powerful Production System* (New York: Productivity Press, 2007).

FIGURE 1.3   Wheel of Waste

Knowledge waste means wasting your time with other waste when you could be improving the business.

Andy taught me that overproduction is the worst form of waste—because it entails every other kind of waste. Again, it made intuitive sense. At the Humpty Dumpty, making more than we could sell was unthinkable, a sure way of going out of business. My parents understand value and waste in their guts, have a deep connection with their customers, and are open to my suggestions for improvement. As a result, the Humpty Dumpty is thriving against tough competition from national restaurant chains.

The jet was passing over Lake Ontario. Way down below, the water was breaking into waves. Soon we'd pass over Toronto, where I had cousins, also in the restaurant business. Then we'd descend into the decaying grandeur that was Detroit.

Our founder, Alfred Taylor, was an acolyte of Henry Ford and had helped to invent the auto industry. We had gone through bad times before, especially in the 1930s and the 1980s when it looked like we might go under. We had always bounced back. But nobody had ever experienced *anything* like the past year.

During the economy's sickening collapse, we lost *40 percent* of our sales. Our president and CEO, John Cafferty, went to Washington cap in hand, to ask for emergency loans. Despite borrowing *$16 billion*, we had to file for bankruptcy protection. The Feds insisted on a radical restructuring plan, and rightly so. So we cut our number of brands and models in half. We cut our dealer network by almost two thirds. Our bondholders have had to accept a debt-for-equity swap that gives them nickels on the dollar. It was a disgrace; many retirees got screwed.

We cut the number of U.S. hourly and salaried employees from about 80,000 to 38,000, and the number of factories from 46 to 22. Each cut is a cry of anguish. I think of how hard our team members work . . . their camaraderie, easy grins, and gentle kidding.

"Hey Tommy, you got a funny walk, man. . . . How do I get a walk like that?"

"You still here, Sidney? I thought they retired your ass . . ."

We emerged from bankruptcy cleansed of the massive debt and crippling contracts that would have sunk us without government loans. We have a clean balance sheet now, a revamped cost structure, and a real shot at redemption. But has our culture changed? Even in freefall, our leadership refused to acknowledge our problems. The Feds had to hold a gun to our heads before we'd consider changing. John Cafferty finally admitted that we *let our customers down*, and asked the public to give Taylor Motors another chance.

John is a man of decency and integrity. He was dealt a terrible hand and I believe has done his best in the circumstances. He's trying to open up decision making in the company. He's reaching out to customers and team members with his blogs. But after 40 years of bad decisions, why should people believe us? Besides, John is outwardly focused. J. Ed Morgan, our CFO, and Fred May, his SVP of Finance, run the company, remote from the customer and factory, absent any understanding, or love, of automobiles.

Morgan is a Yankee aristocrat whose mantra is "Cost walks on two legs." May's an Ivy League goon who terrorizes people through shear meanness and physical size. Execs call it the May Treatment—vicious, unrelenting personal attacks until you give in or leave the company. I can't stand the sonofabitch.

Last year, I made a presentation to the senior leadership team on NJMM's progress. May's body language and demeanor were openly disrespectful. At one point, trying to throw me, I heard him whisper, "This is crap . . ."

I stopped my presentation, walked over to May, and leaned in. "Do you have something to say, Fred?"

The conference room became very quiet. May looked like he'd bitten into a bad cashew. He wasn't used to being challenged, certainly not by a lowly factory manager. "No, I don't have anything to say," he said.

"Good," I said, "then if it's okay with you, I'll resume my presentation."

It wasn't smart politically. May cornered me later, crowding me, glowering at me. "I'm a bad enemy to have, *Papas*."

"You got a problem with my name?"

"I think we had a maid named Papas," he sneered.

"Not likely," I replied. "Greek people don't work for dogs."

I half expected him to attack me. I would've welcomed it. Luckily, my friend and mentor Bill Barrett stepped between us. "Now, now boys, you mustn't curdle the cream."

Rachel Armstrong is Executive Vice President (EVP) of Operations and number three in the company, after Cafferty and Morgan. We call Rachel the "Iron Lady" She loved my confrontation with Fred May. "Thought you were going to tear him a new one!" Soon we'll be calling Rachel the "Digital Lady." She has been advocating the revolution represented by Google for several years now. "It's a new way of thinking," she says, "and we'd better get with it. Customers are in charge. Markets are a dialogue. We need to open up our design process and help customers collaborate with us . . ."

My head spins when Rachel talks that way. John Cafferty's blogs are her idea. Rachel also blogs, twitters, and preaches openness and connectivity—heresy for much of the senior leadership team. Like all car companies, we're secretive about design, cloaking new models like classified weapons.

Before Rachel, we had a series of caretaker executives in operations—old boys, nostalgic for the old days, and coasting to retirement. Rachel came in like a hurricane. She learned the Lean business system working with W. Edwards Deming, the great American quality guru, when she was young. Through Deming, she'd met Shigeo Shingo, Joe Juran, and other greats. She applied their teaching in the auto parts sector and eventually became president of one of our biggest suppliers.

It bugs Rachel when people call Lean a Japanese system. "Henry Ford, Alfred Taylor, Alfred P. Sloan, Peter Drucker, Joe Juran, Ed Deming—do those sound like Japanese names? We respect our Japanese colleagues: the Toyoda family, Soichiro Honda, Taiichi Ohno, and the rest. Andy Saito, our sensei, studied with them and we deeply respect him, too. But this system is not culturally dependent. No reason it can't succeed in America."

Events have proven Rachel's insight. Lean thinking has spread across the world and is no longer just about Toyota and cars. There were brilliant Lean companies all over the place.

Rachel insisted that each factory implement Taylor Motors' version of the Lean business system. My New Jersey plant's overhaul five years ago was a test of Rachel's overall approach. Could a broken-down old brownfield implement the Lean way? If so, Taylor Motors had a chance. If not, Rachel's strategy was questionable—because most of our plants are old, and we can't afford to build new ones. Many executives had bet against Rachel and had been looking forward to her ouster. But as I said, we turned NJMM around, and other plants have improved, too. Much more work to do, but night and day compared to where we were.

Rachel rode shotgun for us. When Morgan conspired to shut down our NJMM transformation, and have me fired, Rachel in turn fired John Sylvain, Morgan's apprentice and my nemesis. Our success vindicated Rachel and put Morgan on the defensive—for now. He and his henchpersons survived the wrecking ball. Their tentacles still constrain the company, not least in the form of our cost-accounting system, that perverse scoreboard that encourages overproduction, and every other kind of waste.

It also bugs Rachel when people call Lean a *manufacturing* system. She loses no opportunity to highlight Lean success stories in fields like health care, financial services, design, retail, and education. Rachel has been trying to push Lean thinking upstream and downstream. "Lean is not a manufacturing system—it's a *business* system. It's about connectivity, transparency, and learning. Lean and Google are *simpatico*."

Rachel has made enemies. Morgan is trying to portray her as rigid and power hungry, which, coming from him, is a joke. But I fear he is setting the stage for another showdown, this time at the board of director level, where he has allies.

I don't care about Morgan or the board. I'm tired of Taylor Motors being a joke. Rachel may be aggressive, but she's right. Fixing our factories isn't enough. We need a remedy for our entire business.

The jet began its descent into Detroit Metro Airport. I looked out over the devastated cityscape. Nature was reclaiming the proud boulevards, handsome homes, and art deco buildings. Weeds and grasses were sprouting through the cracked sidewalks. Deer, coyote, and even beavers had returned. Some people believe it would be a good thing if Detroit disappeared.

I am not one of them.

STUDY QUESTIONS

1. Tom tells us that all he can see upstream and downstream of the factory is "fog." Examples of fog in different business functions are given below—in the form of questions. From your experience, give at least one additional example.

   a. Marketing—What's the purpose of this promotional campaign? How does it relate to our other advertising activities? What were the targets and actual results of the campaign?

   b. Design—What's the capacity of our design studio? What's our current loading? What's our target and actual lead time?

   c. Engineering—What's our current project loading? What's our capacity? What are our most important projects? Are we ahead or behind?

   d. Research and Development—What experiments are we running this week? What phase is each experiment in? What's in the pipeline for next week?

    e. Supply Chain—How many days of finished goods inventory are we carrying? What's our target?

    f. Sales—What's our sales process? How does it adapt to different markets? What skills and skill level do our salespeople need? What skills and skill levels do they actually have?

    g. Human Resources—What are our core HR processes? What are the steps and expected outcomes in each process? How is each process performing?

    h. Finance—Who are the customers of our forecasting process? What does each customer require? How well do we meet each customer's needs?

2. Give an example of each of the following kinds of waste in your organization:

    a. Motion

    b. Waiting

    c. Conveyance

    d. Correction

    e. Overprocessing

    f. Overproduction

    g. Work in Process

    h. Knowledge

3. Who are your *internal* customers?

    a. What do they want from you?

    b. How do you know whether you're meeting their needs?

4. Who are your internal suppliers?

    a. How do you know whether they're meeting *your* needs?

5. Define overproduction. Why is overproduction considered to be the worst kind of waste? Give concrete examples from your industry.

Chapter 2 Lotus Land

I walked out past airport security, picked up my rental car, and got on to Hwy 94. To the west lay the lovely town of Ann Arbor and the University of Michigan, where I'd done my graduate degree. Ann Arbor is an oasis of prosperity, the hub of a network of high technology, health care, and research organizations. I warmly remember its tree-lined streets, splendid campus buildings, and cute coeds.

But I was heading east, toward Taylor City and the epicenter of Michigan's economic meltdown. After a short drive I saw the familiar sign: *Taylor City Next Five Exits*. I pulled off at Lotus Avenue and headed toward the Taylor World Headquarters, an imposing glass-and-chrome building emblazoned with our famous logo. I drove past the old Design Centre and the test track, the Automotive Hall of Fame, and the old Taylor farm, now a museum. On the surface, things looked fine. In fact, many of our buildings were empty.

I parked and walked over to the executive building. We call it Lotus Land; fat salaries and bonuses are its addictive fruit. If there were Oscars for self-absorption, we'd own the Academy Awards. In their blogs, our executives love talking about themselves. But you rarely see the word *customer*.

Security buzzed me through impressive glass doors and invited me to sit down while they contacted Brenda Davies, Rachel's executive assistant. After a few minutes they buzzed me through the next set of doors and directed me to the executive elevators. Brenda was waiting for me at the top floor, elegant and droll, as always. She has a son at Purdue engineering and a daughter at U of M's School of Nursing. Brenda shares Rachel's jaundiced view of corporate life. For some reason, she calls me McDuff, and I call her Mactavish.

"You have arrived McDuff-san," Brenda said.

"I have, Mactavish-san."

I followed Brenda into the heart of Lotus Land: richly paneled hallways, portraits of past presidents, antiques, and elegant offices overlooking the Detroit River. "It's like the Vatican in here," I remarked. Brenda put a forefinger to her lips. "Shush . . . mustn't disturb the massive intellects."

When she was promoted, Rachel got the office next to John Cafferty and J. Ed Morgan. It was my first time seeing it. In fact, there were two offices. The outer one belonged to Brenda and was much nicer than my rat hole at NJMM. Rachel's new dig was a bit smaller than a basketball court. To the left there was a panoramic view of the river; to the right, an enormous tank full of tropical fish. Everywhere else, Michigan oak.

Rachel looked up from her desk and smiled. "*Fish*, can you believe it?"

I laughed. "My dad would put these suckers on the menu. *Mixed grill* . . ."

Rachel got up and gave me a hug. "Good to see you Tommy. How are the girls and Sarah? How are your folks?"

We exchanged pleasantries and caught up on company scuttlebutt. "Hard times," she said, "but much opportunity, too. The dust is starting to settle. If the economy comes back, we've got a real shot."

"People ask me about it every day," I put in. "Are you guys going to make it? We're like Seabiscuit now. The ugly little nag everybody's rooting for."

"Hope you're right, Tom," said Rachel. "Now let's get out of this dump. Bill Barrett's waiting for us at the Design Centre."

We said good-bye to Brenda, went down the elevator and across the street. I always felt good around Rachel. She was a Pittsburgh girl, whose dad had been an hourly worker at the famous Homestead Works, U.S. Steel's flagship plant. For a long time Homestead was the biggest and most productive steel mill in the world. Homestead steel built the New York and Chicago skylines, the Golden Gate Bridge, and the navy that defeated Hitler and Tojo. For a hundred years steel was the greatest business in the world. Then, in a short time, it went to hell.

By the early 1970s the bell was tolling—for anyone who cared to listen. Offshore steelmakers were getting better and better. Initially, they made commodity products like rebar, a segment the major steel companies gave up without a fight. *No margin there.*

In fact, rather than trying to make better steel quicker and at lower cost, the majors tried to keep competitors out with tariffs and the like. It didn't work. The competition began moving up the food chain— into higher margin markets like structural and automotive steel. By the time the major steel makers woke up, it was too late.

People had stopped looking after the mill—and the company. Everybody was stealing, Rachel told me. In the space of five years, an entire industry, and a way of life, collapsed. Rachel's dad got laid off and was never fully employed again. "We'd become middle class," Rachel told me. "Then it was taken from us."

She was the only one of four kids to go to college. It was a fluke, Rachel said. Her parents couldn't afford tuition fees. But one day Rachel read an ad in the paper. Carnegie Mellon Institute was offering free scholarships to qualified kids who could write an essay explaining why they wanted to go to college. Rachel won the scholarship and was on her way. She graduated at the top of her engineering class, overcoming high-voltage sexism.

Rachel joined an auto parts company closely affiliated with Toyota. She excelled and after two decades of achievement became president of North American operations. She joined Taylor Motors seven years ago and last year was promoted to EVP. Her husband, Herb, is a high school principal, a nice fellow who keeps Rachel grounded. They have two grown children.

Rachel is close to her family and loves her hometown. A few years back she asked me to join her on a cross-continent "go-see" of several factories. We took the company jet and, on the way back, stopped in Pittsburgh. Her parents were waiting on the tarmac—good people who'd lived a hardscrabble life, like my folks. After introductions, Rachel invited her folks on to the jet for a tour. They were proud of their precocious daughter, and somewhat in awe. Rachel's mother told us she'd never been on a jet before.

That night I joined Rachel and her family for dinner at a fish joint on Mt. Washington, high above the city. We settled into a booth, ordered drinks, and watched the sun set on the Alleghenies. Way down below us, the Golden Triangle[1] was ablaze, the elegant skyscrapers reflecting the setting sun.

We talked about Pittsburgh's rebirth. In the past 25 years green shoots had sprouted from the barren soil. "Those buildings are now full of pharmaceutical, financial service, and high-tech companies," Rachel said. "We're no longer a steel town."

She pointed out a helicopter flitting over the city. "That's a hospital chopper, likely bringing in cancer patients from out-of-state. Pittsburgh's become an advanced health-care center, too." After that trip, I better understood Rachel's character. And her confidence in Taylor Motor's ability to recover.

Bill Barrett, vice president of manufacturing, was waiting for us at the Design Centre entrance. Bill is a big-bellied Liverpudlian who looks and sounds like *Shrek*. He was the first veteran executive to sign on to Rachel's program. His looks belie a keen mind for manufacturing—and for people. He has survived Taylor Motors' tortuous politics for 30 years. Bill also had my back during NJMM's transformation.

Bill is famous for his one-liners. During an early kaizen, when we were still enamored of Japanese words, he asked, "Tommy, do we really need all this *ninja* stuff?"

He had another one this morning. "All's well, Tom? Box of birds?"

"Box of *what*?"

Rachel rolled her eyes. "Barrett's been collecting cockney slang lately. . . ." Barrett grinned contentedly.

---

[1] Pittsburgh's downtown, at the confluence of the Allegheny River and the Monongahela River whose joining forms the Ohio River.

Rachel led us into the chic new Design Centre with its enormous windows, high atrium, and rust-color walls. We'd completed it last year, just before the economy collapsed. Who knew concrete buildings could be so beautiful?

"We're going to the Defiant design shop," said Rachel. "Follow me."

I raised my eyebrows and looked over at Bill, who started to whistle, trying to look innocent. Why there? The Defiant is a hybrid-electrical vehicle (HEV) we launched a few years back to compete with Toyota's Prius and other "green" cars. It has a great power train comprising a 1.5 litre, 4-cylinder, 80 horsepower engine, continuously variable transmission, nickel-cadmium batteries, and electric motors. But the Defiant hasn't caught on like the Prius has. Delay was a big problem. After months of hype, we kept missing our launch dates. You should see *those* blogs.

We entered a large workroom that had glass walls and a 20-foot ceiling. There were several Defiant sedans on the floor, and fabrication and testing equipment all around. Designers and engineers sat at computers in cubicles on the perimeter.

It wasn't a bad-looking vehicle. HEVs have both an internal combustion engine and an electric motor. They're lighter, cleaner, and more efficient than conventional cars, and have just as much power. We missed the HEV boat a decade ago and are playing catch-up.

"Why are we here?" Rachel began. "Taylor Motors needs to apply Lean thinking in every part of its business. We've done pretty well in manufacturing. Now we need to go upstream and downstream. Frankly speaking, I don't know if it's possible—but if we don't try, we're *toast*."

She let the words sink in. "We also need to do something *extraordinary*, to win back the customer's trust. The two are connected. The former is the *means* to the latter. That's where you come in, Tom. You're one of our best leaders and most original thinkers. Maybe it's because you're a musician, I don't know. Anyhow, we need those qualities now. We also need your tenacity and toughness. You know what we're up against."

"What would you like me to do?" I asked.

Rachel paused and looked over at Bill. "Do you know what a *Shusa* is, Tommy?" Bill asked.

I nodded. "Shusa means heavyweight chief engineer. A Shusa leads an entire automobile platform. They're among the most powerful and respected people in Lean companies."

Bill nodded. "We would like *you* to deploy Lean thinking across an entire platform—by becoming Shusa for the Defiant."

Rachel walked over to the vehicle. "Under your leadership, Tom, NJMM has gone from worst to first. Your Lean Learning Centre has helped improve all our factories. They're world-class now. We're winning that battle but it's not enough. We've got to deploy Lean into *all* our business processes."

Rachel then spoke softly. "Tom, I want you to help us prove that we can manage an entire value stream in a new way."

My head was doing the salsa. How could I apply Lean thinking in business processes I didn't understand? We had only begun this work at NJMM. It was the undiscovered country—full of gold, but also full of drizzle, mud, and fog.

And how could I fulfill the role of Shusa? According to Andy, Shusas or Chief Engineers (CE) "wrap their arms" around an entire platform, and apply the Lean way from voice of the customer, through design, engineering, manufacturing, and supply chain, all the way to the dealer. Shusas are entrepreneurs and system designers at the same time. They break down the silos (see Figure 2.1) that lead to Big Company Disease.

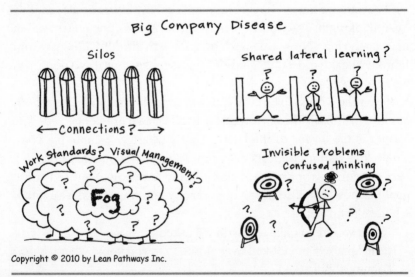

FIGURE 2.1   Big Company Disease

VALUE STREAM THINKING

Taylor Motors, like most organizations, is structured vertically (i.e., by function). This makes sense to people, supports functional excellence, and provides a clear chain of command.

But value flows horizontally. At NJMM, for example, value is created by the interaction between Stamping, Welding, Paint, and Assembly, which transforms raw material into cars. At Taylor Motors as a whole, value is created by the interactions between the silos called marketing, design, engineering, and so on.

How to balance the two? Silo management creates obvious difficulties. But structuring entirely by value stream, as some companies have done, can create its own set of problems (including platform silos!).

Reflection and finesse are required. Our mantra should be "neither too rigid, nor too loose." The approach of many Lean companies is to structure vertically while promoting horizontal collaboration and deep customer consciousness (through the Shusa role, for example).

I walked to a nearby whiteboard and started drawing. "Here's my understanding of the role. The Shusa represents both the customer and the President across the value stream." See Figure 2.2.

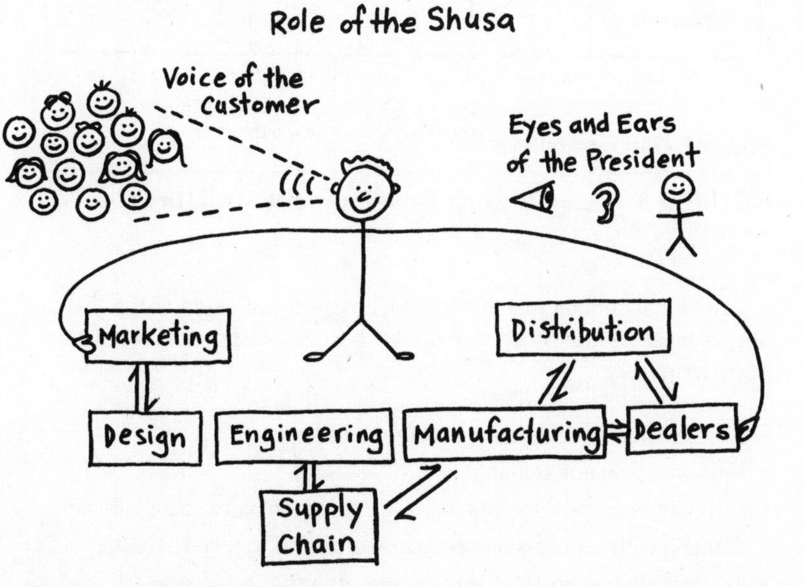

Role of the Shusa

Voice of the Customer

Eyes and Ears of the President

Marketing — Distribution

Design — Engineering — Manufacturing — Dealers

Supply Chain

FIGURE 2.2 Role of the Shusa

"That's a good summary," Bill remarked. "We think it's a good vehicle for deploying Lean across our organization. A decade ago, we created the Platform Leader position. They're supposed to act like Shusas, but they're just bureaucrats, playing the game."

"It's what we reward," said Rachel.

LEAN PRODUCT DEVELOPMENT STRUCTURE AND THE SHUSA

The culture and infrastructure of Lean companies are designed to support cross-functionality (Figure 2.3).

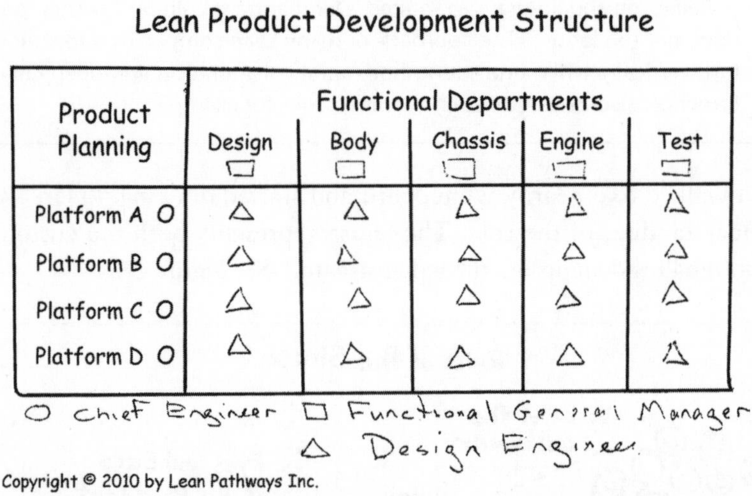

Lean Product Development Structure

Product Planning	Functional Departments				
	Design	Body	Chassis	Engine	Test
Platform A O	△	△	△	△	△
Platform B O	△	△	△	△	△
Platform C O	△	△	△	△	△
Platform D O	△	△	△	△	△

O Chief Engineer   □ Functional General Manager   △ Design Engineer.

Copyright © 2010 by Lean Pathways Inc.

FIGURE 2.3   Lean Product Development Structure

Functional general managers (GMs) make up one side of the matrix, Shusas make up the other. The former have the responsibilities of traditional managers:

- Selection and development of young engineers.
- Performance management.
- Ensuring technical coordination (e.g., common parts across vehicles).
- Working with suppliers on components related to their specialty.
- Assigning engineers to projects run by Shusas.

Functional GMs are also expected to maintain deep technical expertise in their area, develop leadership, and handle all the related administrative work.

The Shusa's job is to make money—by creating profitable platforms. Shusas are aggressive, ornery, and impatient with bureaucracy. They are charismatic, able to communicate a compelling, yet realistic, vision—and inspire disparate teams of people to achieve it. But their vision is guided by engineering and business judgment. They manage consensus and trade-offs while representing the interests of the customer. They're also good at creating simple, effective management systems.

Functional GMs are not responsible for developing the vehicle. That's the job of the Shusa who likewise is not responsible for the administration or for managing engineers. This allows the Shusa to focus on the customer and product, and GMs to focus on managing engineers. Design engineers report to their function's GM, not to the Shusa, who has few direct reports. When engineers work on a design project, they have only a "dotted line" reporting relationship to the Shusa.

But what gives "teeth" to the dotted line? Many companies have matrix structures; most are ineffective because of the "two bosses" syndrome. Why does it work at successful Lean companies? It's a billion-dollar question.

"I think it's a bold idea," I told them. "But I don't think I'm qualified for the job. I know the factory and some of the supply chain. But I *don't* know Marketing, Design, Engineering, or our dealers. It's not my world."

"Not knowing is actually an advantage," Rachel said. "We need fresh eyes, someone who can see all the waste without preconceptions. Tom, you have abundant common sense. You know how to motivate people and how to invent new management methods. That's what we need."

VALUE STREAMS AND VALUE STREAM MAPPING

A value stream is all activities, both value added (VA) and nonvalue added (NVA), required to bring a product or service from order to the hands of the customer, and a design from concept to launch to production to delivery. Value stream mapping is a Lean technique used to
(*continued*)

(*continued*)

analyze the flow of materials and information in a value stream. Some Lean companies called it "material and information" flow mapping. Although value stream mapping is often associated with manufacturing, it is also used in logistics, supply chain, service-related industries, health care, software development, and product development.

Value stream mapping is used to improve lead time and other elements of customer satisfaction by identifying value-added and nonvalue-added steps. For example, at the Humpty Dumpty Bar & Grill, VA activity includes preparing food, pouring drinks, and creating a pleasant eating environment. Most everything else is waste.

Some waste is necessary. For example, waiters have to bring dinner and drinks to your table, but it's still conveyance waste and we have to reduce it where possible. Conveyance waste is a problem at large restaurants. Possible countermeasures include having a minibar, say, on the outdoor patio, so staff don't have to walk all the way to the main bar to fill drink orders.

When analyzing a value stream, it's important to choose the right level of magnification. Too low and you're stuck in the weeds. Too high and you lack the detail needed to make meaningful improvements.

"What about scope?" I asked. "Does the Defiant need radical redesign?"

"It does not, Tom," Bill answered. "That's why we picked it. We call this a *reintegration* project, which means *focused* innovation within an existing platform. The Defiant has a lot going for it. What we need is a handful of innovations and better alignment across the platform."

That was encouraging. Had the project required a breakthrough in, say, hybrid technology, I'd have declined. I don't know enough about it. But I *do* know how to develop management systems and how to focus and align people.

A couple of technologists hooked up equipment to a Defiant and began running tests. Sunlight came in through the glass walls. Rachel and Bill were right to link the assignments. We had to apply Lean thinking outside of our factories, and we needed to make a splash with the customer. The former is indeed the means to the latter. If I could see waste in restaurant and hospital processes, maybe I could do the same in Taylor Motors' business processes. If I had a good team, and Andy Saito as sensei, it just *might* be possible.

"What's the timeline?" I asked.

"SOP^2 is in 12 months," Rachel said. "Then we need to be at full volume within 49 days after that. Our target is to sell 50,000 units the first year and 60,000 second."

It was an aggressive schedule. "Do you have John Cafferty's support?"

"We do," Rachel replied, "but not Morgan's, of course. He says Lean is a factory initiative and our business problems require much more sophisticated solutions. Half the senior leadership team supports us. The rest will fall in line if John is behind it."

It was shaping up as a battle between Rachel and Morgan. Over the past several years she had wrested manufacturing from Morgan's control. Now she was invading our core business processes, Morgan's home turf. If she succeeded, Morgan would be mortally wounded, and Rachel could well be our next president. I knew Morgan was vicious. I remembered his protégé, John Sylvain, and all the trouble he had caused us at NJMM.

"I'd need to be in regular contact with John," I said.

"I'll be your direct contact, Tom. We'll pull in John as required. He'll vigorously promote the project."

"If I'm to be his representative, shouldn't I talk to the guy regularly?"

"John has too much on his plate," said Bill. "He's dealing with the Feds, investors, and the media."

I mulled that one over. "Will the car still be manufactured at CMM?" Connecticut Motor Manufacturing was a good factory located in the green hills just north of New York City. It was commutable for me and I knew its management team well.

"That's right," Bill replied. "CMM is currently on slowdown but we can ramp up quickly. We'll set up a pilot area on-site, and colocate Design and Engineering there. We'd like at lot of the development to happen at CMM."

"Good idea," I told them. "CMM is commutable for me—a bonus. I don't want to be away too much."

---

^{2} Start of project, when the first vehicle comes off the production line.

"We understand that, Tommy." Bill offered. "My guess is you'd be taking several short trips each month, mainly to the head office and to our suppliers. Detroit is easily commutable and most of our suppliers are in the Northeast. We'll support you with a home office, video-conferencing, and whatever else you need."

"I'm feeling overwhelmed," I admitted. "I need to talk to my family."

"Take some time," Rachel said. "Now what say we go for a drive?"

We drove around Taylor City in a cherry red Defiant. Rachel and Bill insisted I take the wheel. I took a left onto Main Street. The farther I drove from Taylor Motors' offices, the more blighted the streets. Our test drive bore out what I'd heard: good powertrain, indifferent styling and interior. The engine was more powerful than I'd expected and very quiet. I liked the multifunction display on the dashboard, which showed accumulated gas mileage and other interesting stuff. XM radio was a nice touch. Mileage was very good, more than 40 miles per gallon.

The Defiant's styling was okay, but that's all. Unlike the Prius, it failed to make a statement. The HID[3] headlights and taillights were a nice touch—but I knew the Prius was going to LED[4] lights. The grill would look great without the chrome above and below. The black mirrors looked rental car cheap. Why not body color or chrome mirrors? The interior felt cramped and had some low-quality plastic. Why not use a decent carbon fiber? I felt the seats were too low and provided inadequate lumbar support. Wind noise, squeaks, and rattles could also be improved. I saw Finance's fingerprints in the poor compromises and false economies.

"It's hard to get excited about this vehicle," I told them when we returned. Rachel and Bill agreed.

---

[3] High-intensity discharge. HID lights offer greater luminance, improved visibility, and longer service life compared to the older halogen lights.

[4] Light-emitting diode lighting, the likely successor to HID lights. LED lights are brighter, have a longer service life, shallower packaging, and offer significant safety benefits.

"No iPod port," said Rachel. "It's a five dollar plug, for heaven's sake . . ."

"One of the many battles we lost with Finance," Bill remarked.

"But the powertrain is good," I said, "and none of these fixes are expensive. Clean them up, get some decent styling, and we've got a winner."

Rachel and I had an early dinner that evening. I had booked a 9 PM flight home. Bill bowed out—granddaughter's concert, he told us. Rachel picked a Lebanese restaurant on Michigan Avenue in Dearborn, not far from Ford headquarters. I drove past the epic Rouge plant, Henry Ford's pride, where so much of modern manufacturing was developed.

Ford, to its credit, has built its most modern facility there, the Dearborn Truck Plant (DTP), a state-of-the-art Lean factory with many environmental innovations, including a "living" roof. I had taken the DTP tour and was impressed. I have quite a few chums at Ford and wish them and the company well.

I found the Pride of Lebanon restaurant, parked, and went inside. It was Friday and the place was starting to fill up. Rachel said she'd be late so I ordered a beer at the bar and kibitzed with the bartender, an engaging old Lebanese with a big nose and bushy eyebrows. "How's business?" I asked.

"Not good," the barkeep replied. "This recession, it stinks! Nobody wants to spend money. Thanks to God, Ford is still in business. Otherwise, we'd be babaghanoush!"

Rachel arrived a few minutes later and we took a quiet table where we could talk. We didn't talk about the job offer. The ball was in my court. She asked me about my band, the Blues Disciples. Still playing monthly gigs, I told her.

Rachel grinned. "If you take this assignment, how will New Jersey's taverns manage?"

"The job would be *painful*—always good for an R&B singer."

Rachel talked about Taylor Motors' bureaucracy and inbred, risk-averse culture, which, she feared, was still intact. John Cafferty was taking steps to change it. He'd eliminated several four-hour meetings, and the premeetings that contributed to glacial decision making. He had dissolved the managerial bottleneck known as the Strategy Board, which in the past had made all significant product and

personnel decisions. Important decisions had often languished, await-
ing the board's monthly meeting.

John now made a point of delegating decisions wherever possible.
He had also simplified Fred May's complex performance measure-
ment system. May, a data-geek, had used more than 10 metrics to
assess executive performance. John boiled them down to five per department, with a much bigger emphasis on sales and profits. Finally,
through his blog and frequent town hall meetings, John was trying
to address the fear that afflicted our culture. He'd even hired a consulting firm to help make our managers less risk averse and more
willing to make decisions. A sad testament to how far Taylor Motors
has fallen.

"We're hoping the Defiant revival project will attract mavericks,"
Rachel said, "people who know to get their ideas past the bureaucracy. We *don't* want the kind of people who wait for signatures."

There were a number of wild cards, Rachel told me. The Feds
were still camped out at our head office—we still owed them a
whack of money. John Cafferty would be closely scrutinized.
Many believed he'd be history if things didn't improve quickly.
Others felt it was a mistake not to take a wrecking ball to the bureaucracy. As I said, I was concerned that Morgan had survived.
In my view, he more than anyone, bore responsibility for the past
20 years.

The board of directors and its new chairman, Warren Arthur Juna,
were another wild card. Art Juna is the first outsider to lead the board
in half a century. He's an ex-marine who made a fortune in the tele-
com business. Juna volunteered for the job, and offered to work for
an annual salary of one dollar, like Lee Iacocca. "I consider it my
duty," he said. Juna vowed to lure the best talent to Taylor Motors so
we could reconnect with customers. He was fully behind the Defiant
revival project.

I was drawn to the challenge, but haunted by the terrible price
Andy had paid. After the trauma of divorce, my life was coming back
together. Sarah was wonderful. We'd been together for five years.
She loved my girls but wanted children of her own. Would I blow it
through blind ambition?

It was a tangled web, and I was in the middle of it (see Figure 2.4).

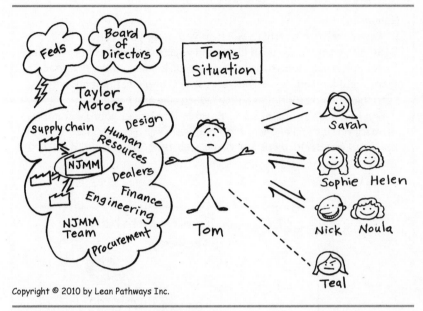

Copyright © 2010 by Lean Pathways Inc.

FIGURE 2.4   Tom's Situation

WHERE DO WE START?

Taylor Motors is several years into its journey and is ready for more advanced Lean concepts such as value streams and Shusas. But what if your organization is just beginning to implement Lean? Here are some questions to get you going:

- Who are our customers?
- What do they value? (What do they expect from us?)
- Who are our suppliers? (What do we expect from them?)
- What are our most important processes for delivering value to our customers?
- What are the steps in each process? Which ones add value, and which ones do not?
- What kind of waste do we see in our current processes?
- How might we reduce waste?

(continued)

(continued)

Answering such questions will help you grasp your current situation. Next, ask where do we need to be, and what's stopping us from getting there? Pull in Lean tools to address the obstacles. Remember Andy Saito's guideline: No need, no activity! Mechanical implementation is aimless. Lean thinking and tools stick if they reduce pain and hassle.

Figure 2.5 gives one of many possible trajectories your Lean implementation might take. There is no one best way. For a detailed illustration of a Lean deployment, see *Getting the Right Things Done: A Leader's Guide to Planning and Execution* by yours truly.

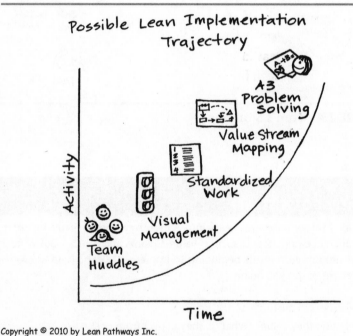

Copyright © 2010 by Lean Pathways Inc.

FIGURE 2.5 Possible Lean Implementation Trajectory

STUDY QUESTIONS

1. What are *three* value streams in your organization?
   a. Draw out all the steps in *one* of these value streams.
   b. Mark the value-added and nonvalue-added steps in each value stream.
2. What are some of the advantages of organizing by function (e.g., Design, Engineering, Operations, Finance)?
   a. What are some of the disadvantages?
3. What are some of the advantages of organizing by value stream (e.g., by car model in a car making company)?
   a. What are some of the disadvantages?
4. Give three examples of fear in an organization.
5. What creates fear in an organization?
6. How do we dispel fear in an organization?

Chapter 3 What Have I Learned?

Sarah was still awake when I returned to our apartment in Hoboken. She made us drinks and we sat out on the balcony overlooking the Hudson River and the New York skyline, which always thrilled me. Be daring, it whispered. Life is short.

It was a soft summer night. A tugboat worked its way up the Hudson River. Sarah listened quietly as I recounted the day's events. "Sounds like it's an amazing opportunity—and a lot of work. Are you ready to work that hard again?"

Unspoken was our unfinished conversation. *Would we marry? Would we have children?* We'd been together five years. It was decision time. There were other questions, too. Would Sophie and Helen be okay with a little brother or sister? Would it affect my relationship with my ex-wife? If I took a killer job, would I have the energy to help Sarah?

"I'm ready to work hard," I replied. "Just want to make sure it doesn't become all-consuming. Know what I mean?"

Sarah topped up our wineglasses. "I know what you mean. Glad you're thinking about it."

The next day was Saturday and I drove across town to my ex-wife's apartment on the Upper East Side to pick up my girls. It's a fine old building with a nice fountain outside and an elegant foyer. Chris the doorman, a fellow Greek, has silver hair and a fine moustache. "Yiasou, levendi," he said. Our plan was to meet Sarah at the Humpty Dumpty for lunch, and then go bike-riding in Astoria Park.

I called Teal on the way and told her about the job offer. "If I took it, I'd be traveling more. It'd put more strain on you. Occasionally, we'd have to adjust my midweek visits with the girls."

Teal surprised me. "I think it's an important opportunity, Tom. I think you should go for it. We'll work out your visits with the girls." I hadn't heard her use that tone of voice in a long time. Gone was the edge, the sarcasm that I'd always found so difficult. "Thanks," I told her. "Means a lot to me."

The girls and I said good-bye to mommy and took the elevator down to the lobby and our car. As we drove, Sophie and Helen recounted their adventures the past week. I told them about my trip to Detroit and Rachel's proposal.

"It sounds like a very important job, daddy," my beautiful, logical Helen said.

"Yeah, and I bet they give you a new car," said Sophie, my practical jitterbug.

"If you take the job, will we still see you?" Helen asked.

"Of course you will," I replied. "No job will take me away from you."

"Then it's okay with us," Sophie said.

We took a detour down Fifth Avenue, so we could drive past Central Park. We passed the Jackie Onassis Reservoir, the Guggenheim gallery and the Metropolitan Museum of Art. New York was drenched in April sunshine. People were smiling, cherry trees were in bloom.

What did Teal's tone of voice mean? After the trauma of divorce, was a different kind of relationship possible? After all the terrible strife, could we let go of the past? I was afraid to get my hopes up.

I took the 59th Street Bridge across the East River and into Queens. I made a left at 31st Street and we were in Astoria, the streets where I grew up. I pointed out the landmarks for Sophie and Helen. "There's

Holy Name High School and the parish hall where daddy played stickball. There's Athens Bakery and Christos Billiards. There's Saint Irene's where you were baptized!"

"We know, Daddy."

"And there at the corner of Ditmars and 31st . . ."

"The Humpty Dumpty!"

"WELCOME, WELCOME, WELCOME!" said my dad when we walked in. He was wearing his chef's hat and apron. Mama was wearing her waitress uniform. "Ti kanete, my little angels," she said. The girls ran up and embraced their grandparents. I gave Mama and Dad a kiss.

"You must be starving," Mama said. "The lamb is good today. How about some meze and a glass of wine? We just got a shipment of white from Santorini."

We sat in an orange booth with a blue-checkered tablecloth and took in the Humpty Dumpty's goofy splendor. Spin-around stools and the long Formica counter, Corfu travel posters and corny celebrity photos. Uncle Louie was cracking jokes with the regulars. Sunlight poured in through the big front window.

When Sarah joined us my parents made a big fuss. "You look beautiful, my dear," Mama said, "but maybe a bit thin. Are you eating enough?"

"WHAT DO YOU MEAN THIN? SARAH IS TOPS, SHE IS NUMBER ONE! AREN'T YOU, MY DEAR?"

Sarah took it in with her usual grace and good humor. At first, I was afraid my folks would be too much for her. Don't worry, she laughed, my parents are crazy Hungarians. After lunch Mama made thick Greek coffee and I told everybody about Rachel's offer.

"It sounds like a wonderful opportunity, chriso mou," Mama put in. "But I don't like you traveling too much. These airplanes, they're not safe."

"I'd be taking short trips to Detroit and to suppliers around the Northeast," I said. "I'm more concerned about the job itself. I don't know if I'm up to it."

"TOMMY, PAIDI MOU, FOR YOU NOTHING IS IMPOSSIBLE! REMEMBER WHEN THEY WERE GOING TO SHUT DOWN THE NEW JERSEY FACTORY? WHO SAVED IT? TOM PAPAS! AND WHY? BECAUSE YOU ARE A PHENOMENA!"

Nick Papas has a way with words. Phenomena, spelled with an a, was one of my favorites. "Thanks, Dad," I said. "But this'll be a lot harder than turning a factory around. We'll have to improve the whole company."

"Will that nice Japanese man help you, Tommy?" Mama asked.

"Hope so," I replied. "I'm going to call Andy this weekend. I'm concerned he might say no, given Toyota's current problems."

"I hope Andy says yes," Mama said, "I don't want you doing this all by yourself. You have a responsibility to the children—and to Sarah."

After we finished our coffee, Sarah and I turned over our cups so Mama could read our fortunes in the coffee grinds. Looking into mine, she said, "I see a long journey . . ."

If I wanted the job, I had my family's support. As ever, they were putting my needs first. When we got home that night, I called Andy Saito. He listened quietly then suggested we have dinner at the Iron Horse, our regular hangout near NJMM. "Shall we meet at the factory?" I asked.

"How about we meet at a Taylor Motors dealership?" Andy responded. "I believe there is one not far from the factory."

The following week I drove out of the NJMM parking lot and headed to Bill Quigley's, an old, established dealership that had survived the purges of the past year. Dealers are a sore spot in the car business. State franchise law prohibits us from selling directly to the public, so we *have* to sell through dealers. But the public doesn't trust them. In fact, more and more people want to buy cars online. Andy told me that Toyota also has problems with their U.S. dealer network.

"The Lean Management System has three elements," Andy told me. "Design, Production, and Sales. North American companies focus on the Production side of system. But Design and Sales are just as important!"

I drew it out in my notebook. I'd learned the "house of Lean production" (Figure 3.1). Now I needed to learn about the design and sales part of the system (Figure 3.2).

We'd had a good production day and had met our throughput targets with no injuries and no overtime. We'd had some quality problems though, which we'd contained, but hadn't resolved. At our daily shipping quality audit, my parting words were, "We're not even *close* to root cause yet."

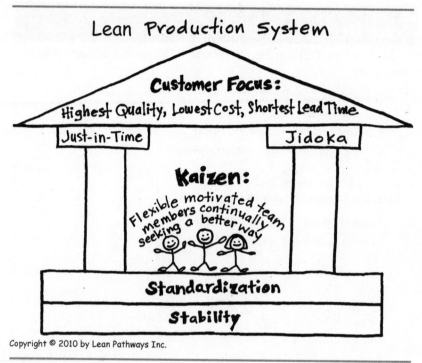

Copyright © 2010 by Lean Pathways Inc.

FIGURE 3.1   Lean Production System

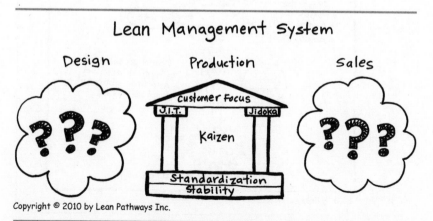

Copyright © 2010 by Lean Pathways Inc.

FIGURE 3.2   Lean Management System

FOUR-STEP PROBLEM SOLVING

The Four-Step Problem Solving Process (4SPS) entails answering four questions:

1. Do I have a problem?
2. Do I know the cause?
3. Have I confirmed cause and effect?
4. Have I confirmed the countermeasure?

Figure 3.3 illustrates the process.
Question 1 entails answering two questions:

1. What should be happening?
2. What is actually happening?

Question 2 entails applying Lean's famous Five Why Analysis to find:

- Point of Cause—the physical time and location at which the abnormality is first observed.
- Direct Cause—usually one Why removed from the point of cause.

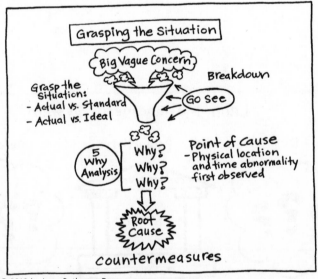

FIGURE 3.3 Problem-Solving Funnel

- Root cause—usually (a) inadequate standard, (b) inadequate adherence to standard, or (c) inadequate system.

Question 3 entails running rapid experiments to confirm you've found the root cause.

Question 4 entails implementing defect-proofing, visual management, and other Lean tools to ensure that the problem does not recur.

Here's a Humpty Dumpty Bar & Grill example of getting to the root cause.

Problem: The Cheese-less Cheeseburger

Do I have a problem? Yes!

- What should be happening? I should have cheese on my burger!
- What's actually happening? No cheese!

Do I know the cause?

- Point of cause: Hey, there's no cheese on my burger!
- Direct Cause:
  - Why? Because the cook didn't put cheese on it.
  - Why? Because he ran out of cheese.
  - Why? Because the supplier didn't bring any cheese.
  - Why? Because we didn't ask him to.
  - Why? Because we didn't know we were out of cheese.
  - Why? Because visual management in our stock room and our replenishment process with suppliers is substandard.

This is the root cause. To fix it we have to go to steps 3 and 4 in our problem-solving process.

Note: To download the problem-solving funnel, please go to www.leanpathwaysinc.com/templates.

I was being hard on my team, which is what they need right now. People think a Lean workplace is a Shangri-la. *Not true.* It's intense, fast-paced, and hard-nosed, kind of like playing hockey in the NHL.[1] Everybody is fast, tough, and a good puck handler. Reality, in the form of major problems, often creams you into the boards, and thereby reveals the weaknesses in your management system. You have to pick yourself up and skate back into the play. Each company implementing Lean has to ask, "What's the right intensity level for us?"

---

[1] National Hockey League.

I don't want to be misunderstood. A Lean workplace is also fun, rewarding, and deeply satisfying. I remember something Bonny, one of our Assembly team leaders, told me at a report out. "Tom, I don't ever want to go back to how we were!"

"Why is that, Bonny?"

"Cause I don't *ever* want to live in a box again!"

One of Andy's greatest lessons was his focus on safety. "To make good car Tom-san," he had told me, "we need four *M*s: man and woman, machine, material, and method. The first *M* is the most important. If we do not take care of team member, we cannot make a good car."

Our commitment to safety had cemented our relationship with our union and helped to engage 2,000 team members. Moreover, safety had given us a bridge to broader improvement. Safety problems, such as bad ergonomics on an assembly line, always mean quality, delivery, and cost problems as well. Could we find a galvanizing element for the Defiant platform, to play the role safety had played in the factory?

The first year of our transformation Andy spent a few days per week at the plant, giving us assignments and checking on previous assignments. His philosophy was "learn by do." In the second and third years, he reduced his visit frequency to one per month. Now Andy was visiting us once a quarter.

Had it really been five years? I had filled several thick notebooks with reflections, charts, and doodles. Many people thought the Lean system was a set of tools. They were *wrong*. Elegant Lean tools like 5 S, standardized work, quick changeover, and kanban[2] were simply *countermeasures* to specific problems.

Some companies had integrated the tools into a management system— a sensible idea. So now, in addition to the Toyota Management System, we have the Ford Production System (FPS), the Alcoa Business System (ABS), and others.

But underlying the tools and management system, is a *way of thinking*. Here's a corresponding Lean mantra: *Good thinking, good products*. See Figure 3.4.

---

[2] For a detailed discussion of Lean thinking and tools, the reader is referred to *Lean Production Simplified: A Plain Language Guide to the World's Most Powerful Production System*, by yours truly (New York: Productivity Press, 2007).

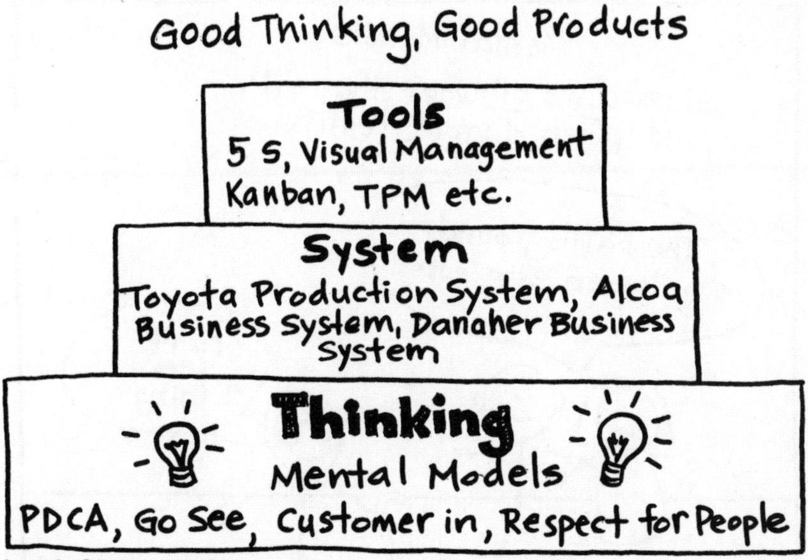
Good Thinking, Good Products
Tools
5 S, Visual Management
Kanban, TPM etc.
System
Toyota Production System, Alcoa Business System, Danaher Business System
Thinking
Mental Models
PDCA, Go See, Customer in, Respect for People
Copyright © 2010 by Lean Pathways Inc.

FIGURE 3.4 Good Thinking, Good Products

Early in NJMM's transformation, Andy had asked our leadership team: You have learned to think in a certain way over many years. How will you change your thinking?

The question haunts me. The battleground is between our ears. The bad news: It's hard to change thinking—the result of temperament, upbringing, education, and experience. The good news: If we can change our thinking, we have a nonreplicable competitive advantage.

So we need to understand, and deepen, our mental models, the glasses we all wear, which filter, and often distort, reality. Two people walk into the Humpty Dumpty—and pick out different faces. Same sensory data—different perceptions. Reality is subjective; the world we see is our own (see Figure 3.5).

My job as a leader is to continually illuminate blind spots, mine and those of my team, so we can *see what's there*. Start by getting off your duff and out to the *gemba*—the real place where what matters happens. The gemba for a designer might be the wind tunnel, factory, or customer's garage. The marketer's gemba includes the dealership, TV spot seen in the local bar, or the park the soccer dad drives his kids to. The engineer's gemba might include the prototype shop, test track, or

FIGURE 3.5   Mental Models

factory. Nothing beats direct observation. Don't trust the computer screen, report, or phone message. *Genchi genbutsu*—Go see for yourself!

Go see doesn't mean milling around aimlessly. You go with a purpose, a clear understanding of your "hot spots," and with your intuition primed. You thereby engage both your left and right brains—the analytical and creative parts, respectively. Thus, you begin to *grasp the situation (GTS)*, which means understanding what should be happening, what's actually happening—and *why*.

Then we can ask meaningful questions. What problem are we trying to solve? How do we know that's the real problem? What assumptions have we made? What if our assumptions weren't true? What's the cause of the problem? How can we prove cause and effect? What experiments might we run? How will we confirm our countermeasures?

I remember a kaizen workshop[3] we ran at a parts supplier, where Andy gave me a lesson in GTS. Andy asked me to find out what they make. I came back later in the day with a list. "How did you get that info?" Andy asked. I explained that I'd talked to the production manager. Andy frowned. "Do you really know? Please go see again." So I came back later that day with another list. "How do you know this is what they make?" Andy asked. I told him that I'd gone to the supplier's accounting department to see what had been invoiced as shipped. "But how do you know this is what they make?" Andy asked.

So I went back to accounting and asked to see what Taylor Motors had actually paid for. I couldn't imagine that we'd pay for parts we hadn't received. When I showed him the list, Andy shook his head. "You still don't know."

I came back the next day with a different list. It had taken longer but this time I felt I was ready. "How do you know this is what they make?" Andy asked. I told him I'd stood in shipping and recorded every box that was loaded onto the truck for delivery. I'd written down the part number stamped on the part, as well as, the shipping label. I'd also confirmed that there was a machine in the plant that could make that part. Not that I suspected the supplier was reselling us parts made by someone else—but now I had verified it.

Andy looked at the list, and at me, and finally nodded. "Okay, not bad. Next question. How are these parts made?"

A wise man[4] once said, "Culture isn't just part of the game—it is the game." So what is culture? Day-to-day behavior.

And what determines day-to-day behavior? How we think.

Here are some things I've learned.

Plan-Do-Check-Adjust

W. Edwards Deming's Plan-Do-Check-Adjust (PDCA) cycle is a practical expression of the scientific method and the engine of the Lean management system. These four words are easy to say. Andy once

---

[3] Kaizen workshops are focused improvement activities involving small cross-functional teams in the gemba. Their purpose is to solve the problem, and to *learn* how to solve problems.

[4] Lou Gerstner, former CEO of IBM.

told me it took him 40 years to learn PDCA. He also told me, "A manager's job is to practice and teach PDCA."

I've made many PDCA doodles over the years. See Figure 3.6.

Customer-In Mentality

Customer-in mentality entails a shared commitment to the customer. This means the external *and* internal customer, usually the process downstream to yours. Thus, manufacturing is design's customer, just as design is marketing's customer. Customer-in thinking guides you through the minefield of trade-offs every business faces. Simply asking, "Is this good for the customer?" can by itself resolve difficult decisions. See Figure 3.7.

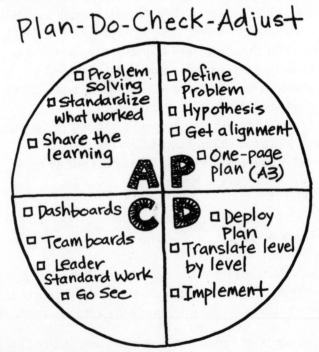

FIGURE 3.6 Plan-Do-Check-Adjust

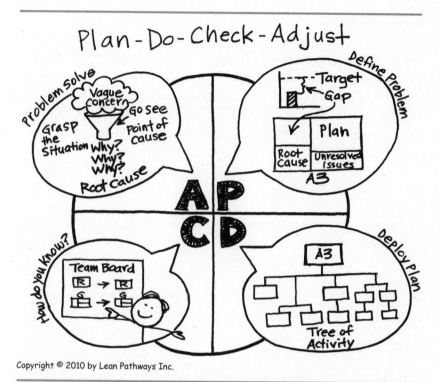

FIGURE 3.6   Plan-Do-Check-Adjust (continued)

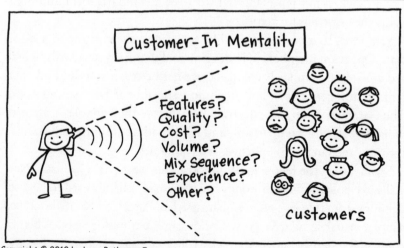

FIGURE 3.7   Customer-In Mentality

Respect for People

I've learned that people want to do a good job. Respect their human-
ity, treat them like adults, and you can tap into a mother lode of
energy and ideas. Do you have troublemakers in your organization?
Engage them in work planning and design and watch what happens.
Occasionally you get a bad pomegranate, but it's rare.

Simple Visual Standards

We have simple visual standards for all important things. Standardized work comprises:

- Content
- Sequence
- Timing
- Expected outcome

It should also contain tests, or red flags, which tell you when there's
a problem. That way, you won't ship junk. The tests could be physical, such as a torque check on a bolt, or it could be administrative,
like a blacked-out template that fits over a standard form and high-
lights the critical information.

Standards to a company are like scales and sheet music to a musician. Our team members help develop and maintain standards, which
are *not* static. Standards change as we get better, just as a good band
will incorporate chord and melodic variations if they sound good.
Thus, standards do *not* constrain creativity—they enable it, by providing a basis for comparison, and by providing stability, so we have
the time and energy to improve. See Figure 3.8.

Sarah has a little fellow in her kindergarten class who is autistic. New
skills like going to the bathroom and washing his hands used to be difficult for Carlos. He was often embarrassed and upset. So Sarah developed
simple, visual standards. Now Carlos can see things clearly. When he
completes a step, he moves the Velcro dot to the next step in the process.
Result: No more accidents and a happier, more confident child. When
I commended Sarah, she was puzzled. "Doesn't everybody do this?"

Copyright © 2010 by Lean Pathways Inc.

FIGURE 3.8   Standards

Visual Management

We want to satisfy the "visual management triangle" with simple visual tools like scoreboards, charts, and traffic lights. Here's a good test: Does everybody understand what's going on? Sarah understands this intuitively. Her class is full of charming visual management, which makes it a fun and interesting place. See Figure 3.9.

Problems Are Treasure

Problems are gold to be treasured, not garbage to be buried. Problems are the process talking to us, telling us where our management system is weakest. We need to use our stethoscopes to probe deeper, get to the root cause, and fix it. If we tune out problems, we're lost.

Before Andy, our NJMM meetings focused on the good news. Now we focus on the bad news. Here are some corollaries:

- Really good companies don't think they're good—because they are acutely aware of their problems.
- Bad companies think they're good—because they're oblivious to their problems.

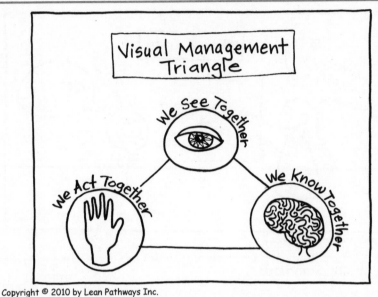

FIGURE 3.9 Visual Management Triangle

This is most obvious in sports. Truly great teams are humble and reflective. After a victory players talk about things they could've done better. See Figure 3.10.

FIGURE 3.10 Problems Are Treasure

Flow

Make stuff and provide service *one unit at a time*, instead of in big batches. The simplest way to get flow is to put all the value-added steps elbow to elbow with one unit of inventory in between. That's how Dad and Uncle Louie assemble burgers, sandwiches, and salads, with the following benefits:

- They can spot *quality* problems, like stale bread, at once, instead of finding them after making a batch of 50.
- *Delivery time* is reduced because the customer doesn't have to wait for the entire batch to be completed.
- *Cost* is also reduced because we don't have to buy more supplies than we need.

To sustain flow you've got to continually reduce waste and variation in your process, which means continually improving standards, visual management, and training.

Pull

Provide the product or service in the volume, sequence, and mix in which the customer withdrew it. We've developed a nice pull system in the Humpty Dumpty stockroom. Shelves are clearly labeled so at a glance you can tell:

- What is it?
- Where is it?
- How many (i.e., min/max level)?

Kanbans are attached to each storage location with Velcro. When we hit the minimum level of, say, tomato sauce or broccoli, we pull the kanban and put it in a clear plastic sleeve on the stockroom door. At the end of each day Uncle Louie collects the kanbans and restocks accordingly. The benefits to the business include fresher food, lower bills, and less storage space.

Kanbans help connect customers and suppliers who are physically isolated. When they're elbow to elbow, suppliers can see what customers are consuming. When an organization gets big, the anaesthetizing fog of complexity drifts in.

Jidoka

Build quality into each process; don't ship junk. Stop the process when junk is discovered, get to the root cause, and fix it, so the process does not have to stop again. Junk is visible in a factory—a pile of substandard car bodies is hard to miss. But junk in business processes is *invisible*. Who can tell if an engineering drawing meets the standard? How would you know if a forecast was faulty? See Figure 3.11.

Yokoten

Share knowledge across the company through mutual, experiential learning. Yokoten is one of the antidotes to Big Company Disease. In

Copyright © 2010 by Lean Pathways Inc.

FIGURE 3.11 Jidoka—Don't Ship Junk!

fact, if you share learning, a big company's scale becomes an advantage! What you learn in, say, Brazil is likely applicable in China. You don't have to repeat mistakes. Lean companies learn exponentially—through yokoten.

I like Rachel's focus on information technology and her embrace of Google. It's not sufficient, in my view. The heart of yokoten is personal experience in the gemba with a capable sensei. Without Andy at my elbow, I wouldn't have learned as much and as quickly. Our challenge is coming up with learning channels that replicate what NJMM and I experienced with Andy.

Leader = *Sensei*

A leader's job is to build capability—of people, processes, and machinery. The leader asks questions, as Socrates did in the agora of ancient Athens, so that we can understand what's wrong and how to improve. See Figure 3.12.

Leaders should be judged, therefore, by the footprint they leave. Are people, processes, and machine systems stronger than when they arrived? Can the organization run itself in the leader's absence?

FIGURE 3.12   Leader = Sensei

This is a big problem for Taylor Motors. Our human resources system is chaotic. I hesitate to call it a system in fact. It seems more like a bunch of random activities with a veneer of complexity to discourage questions.

Kaizen

Every day we get a little bit better. We seek perfection, knowing we'll never achieve it. That's okay. The *journey* is the point—not the destination. A Buddhist friend says that Buddhism encourages a continuous, humble striving to get better, as well as an acceptance of what *is*; in other words, where you currently are. If so, this may help explain why Asian companies pioneered Lean. Some people suggest that Western culture and religion are less amenable to continuous improvement. I don't buy it.

Andy had a nice expression: *Every day a little up*. See Figure 3.13.

FIGURE 3.13   Every Day a Little Up

I'm deeply grateful to Andy, and to Toyota, for freeing him up. Without his help we would have lost NJMM and 2,000 jobs. Taiicho Ohno, Eiji Toyoda, and the rest created a manufacturing revolution. When they realized its power, they shared it with the world. My respect for them knows no bounds.

Now Lean thinking is spreading outside of manufacturing and creating breakthroughs in health care, financial services, construction, education, and even in government. It made sense. If Lean works in a Greek restaurant, it'll work anywhere. Lean companies are usually open about their methods and invite other companies into their sites to learn. Toyota even launched a joint venture with General Motors in California in 1982—a great learning opportunity for GM. It took GM a while to internalize the lessons, but now their factories are as good as any in the world.

Taiichi Ohno was Andy's sensei for several years when Andy worked at Operations Management Consulting Division (OMCD), Toyota's internal consulting group. I love Andy's stories about the early days. There were few epiphanies, just continuous experimentation and a commitment to getting better each day.

"Ohno-san was a severe sensei." Andy told me. "He always tried to create a positive tension in the workplace. *'You can't hire more people! You'll have to make do with the machines you have! You are getting complacent. Cut your inventory in half!'* Over time I realized that Ohno-san's chief interest was not raising productivity, improving quality, or lowering cost. His ultimate goal was to help people achieve their potential."

That one stayed with me. *What kind of a man was Taiichi Ohno?* Andy showed me old photos of Ohno on the factory floor. Moustache, supervisor's cap and tie, hands on his hips, trying out stuff. He exuded toughness and good humor. Like Deming, Ohno had no patience with bureaucrats, and almost got himself fired a number of times. But Eiji Toyoda always covered for Ohno and attended to the ruffled feathers and egos in his wake. See Figure 3.14.

I parked in front of Bill Quigley's dealership and went inside. Andy was waiting for me, a smiling Japanese man of medium height, with hawk eyes, high cheekbones, and a moustache. His hair was streaked with silver, his demeanor endearingly childlike. We shook hands.

If they're to reach their potential, I'm going to have to push these jokers....

Taichii Ohno

Copyright © 2010 by Lean Pathways Inc.

FIGURE 3.14   Taiichi Ohno

"Konnichiwa, Tom-san!"

"Konnichiwa, sensei. Okegi desu ka?"

"I am very well, thank you. Your accent is getting better!"

"Thanks. Must be all the years I spent at New York Aikikai[5]—getting my butt kicked."

Andy grinned and motioned around him. "If you accept Rachel-san's offer, this will be your *gemba*![6] What do you think, Tom-san?"

It looked like a typical dealership. Things were busier than I expected. Salespeople were taking prospective buyers out for test drives. Others were doing paperwork. In the Service Area lounge a number of people were waiting to pick up their vehicles.

"It's very different than a factory," I said. "Strange that I know so little about our dealerships."

Andy walked over to a Defiant on display. He walked around the car, scrutinizing paint quality and body panel fit. He opened the doors and looked over the interior trim and dashboard. "What do you think of the Defiant, Tom-san?"

---

[5] Aikido is a Japanese martial art. Aikikai means aikido club.

[6] *Gemba* means "real place" or "place where the real work gets done" in Japanese.

"I took it for a drive in Taylor City. Good powertrain, so-so styling. I find the interior cramped and unappealing. Body panel fit is sloppy—too much wind noise. Assembly could be better—too many squeaks and rattles. Oh, and I don't like the name. *Defiant* sends the wrong message to our customers. We've just come out of bankruptcy. We should be on bended knee asking customers for a chance to regain their trust."

Andy listened closely. A salesman walked over and asked if he could help us. I didn't tell him who we were. He was a nice kid and told us what he knew about the vehicle. We went out for a test drive, Andy at the wheel. When we asked about price, the salesman was evasive. He quoted an overly high number then suggested we might be able to "work something out." This was a problem. Most people hated haggling with car salespeople.

The kid gave us his card, some sales pamphlets, and said please feel free to call. I looked over at the service area. Looked like the same people were still there waiting for their vehicles.

Andy and I walked down the street to the Iron Horse for dinner. We greeted the crew there and took our usual table. Margie sidled over with a couple of menus. "Howdy gentlemen! Mr. Saito, long time no see."

"Howdy, Margie-san," Andy said, "New Jersey factory team is improving. They don't need Saito-san every week. More time for gardening!"

Margie started us off with bourbon on the rocks, and told us about the specials. Running Toyota's flagship Kentucky plant, Andy had developed a taste for bourbon, which he passed on to me. We ordered dinner and settled in.

Andy looked at me keenly. "Impressions of the dealership, Tom-san?"

I took a pull on my drink. "My biggest impression is, *This doesn't feel like part of Taylor Motors.* Other impressions: The salesman didn't know the car that well. Was he following a sales process? It wasn't clear. I didn't like the vagueness about price. Also, there was a big queue in the service department and it wasn't moving."

"What kind of muda did you see? What do you think is the cause?"

"I saw *delay* waste in the service area, which could be caused by *overprocessing* waste—like too many handoffs for a work order.

Delay could also be caused by inadequate cross-training of mechanics, which means *knowledge* waste, or by a defective scheduling process, which often means *rework* waste. Delay could be caused by part stock-outs, likely caused by *excessive* inventory—another waste. The last is one of many paradoxes you've taught us. . . ."

Andy nodded, and then added his own observations, which went much deeper than mine. As always, I was amazed at how much he had seen. To me, Andy seemed a Sherlock Homes of management, diagnosing deep system problems from clues invisible to most of us.

Margie brought us dinner and more bourbon. "Will you accept Rachel's assignment?" Andy asked, sampling his steak-and-kidney pie.

"I wanted to speak with you first." I said. "The Defiant project does *not* require breakthrough innovation in design or engineering. Rachel calls it a 'reintegration' project, which means we keep the basic design and make a handful of *focused* innovations. But it will require breakthroughs in the *design* process. In a nutshell, this means we have to implement Lean thinking across the platform. My gut tells me it's doable—if you'll help us."

I paused. Would Andy help a rival company, when Toyota was in such difficulty?

Andy took a pull on his bourbon. "I have spoken with my colleagues in Toyota City. They have encouraged me to help you."

I was humbled. With all their difficulties, Toyota was still prepared to help a rival company. Their hoshin was to make the world a better place. Maybe they actually mean it.

"Thank you, sensei," I said. "I couldn't imagine taking this on without you." Andy bowed.

"But there's something bothering me," I went on. Am I *capable* of being a Shusa? I'm a factory manager. What do I know about marketing, design, procurement, and dealerships?"

"It will be a big challenge for you. But if you have a good team and senior management support, you have a good chance."

"This is way harder than transforming a factory," I reflected. "Taylor Motors has a lot of baggage, a history of bad thinking, especially outside the factory. We'll face enormous obstacles."

Andy nodded. "We must *try*. Taylor Motors' manufacturing is much better now. The biggest problems are now *outside* of manufacturing.

There are many talented people. If we can focus and align, we can succeed."

Andy and I made a list of what we'd need:

- Visible support by John Cafferty and the senior leadership team. Regular communication with Cafferty and Rachel.
- Functional general managers and executives free up their best people to support Lean implementation across the Defiant program; target complement: one Lean leader per 300 team members.
- Performance metrics adjusted to reflect the importance of supporting the Defiant program.
- Tom Papas chooses a team of six people. (Initially, I wanted ten people. "Too many," Andy said.)
- Joe Grace, my assistant plant manager at NJMM, becomes acting plant manager in my absence.
- At the end of the project, I have the right to return to my old job if I want to.
- Tom Papas has the right to change the name of the vehicle.

I shared the list with Rachel and she agreed at once. She reminded me that *she* would be my daily contact point, not Cafferty. She acknowledged my concerns about Cafferty's engagement with the project.

Rachel was delighted and relieved that Andy had agreed to support us. She and Andy worked out terms of engagement. Rachel sent gracious, handwritten thank-you notes, both to Andy to the executives in Toyota City who had encouraged his involvement. I negotiated a healthy raise and bonus.

"What shall we call you?" Rachel asked. "I'm not sure the term *Shusa* will resonate. *Platform Leader* certainly won't work, given our history."

"How about Entrepreneurial System Designer?"

Rachel made a face. "I know that describes the job, but good God . . . How about something simple, like Chief Engineer?"

"Okay by me," I replied. We clinked glasses.

"You know what bothers me about the Defiant?" Rachel said. "It doesn't have a *soul*. Give the car a soul, Tommy."

I flew to Motown the following week for John Cafferty's monthly Town Hall meeting, broadcast across the Net to all team members. I sat up on the dais in the old auditorium with Rachel and J. Ed

Morgan. John began by welcoming everybody and summarizing the month's business results.

I've never connected with John Cafferty. He's a brilliant man, but I sense a certain coldness, a wall. At times he seems to fade in and out of focus. Yet I also sense integrity and decency. Maybe it comes with being CEO. John is the public face of Taylor Motors, meeting with investors, analysts, and, of course, the Feds. As I said, Morgan runs the business. So everything John does is magnified a thousand times. I guess you learn to cover up.

Now John was talking about the Defiant project, the Chief Engineer's role, and what Lean meant for Taylor Motors. "I genuinely believe that Lean is our future. We've done well in our factories. Now we have to deploy this powerful management system across our company. The Defiant new model launch is our chance to do that. Tom Papas will be my eyes and ears. And more important, he'll be the voice of the customer. Please support him. Let's show the world that Taylor Motors is back."

John then handed me the microphone and asked me to say a few words. I looked into the camera. I had never spoken to thousands of people before. Something crystallized in me. We would succeed at this project beyond any possibility of doubt. I would not compromise, play the game, or praise the emperor's new clothes.

"I've been at Taylor Motors my entire career," I began. "Twenty years of getting our butts kicked. I'm tired of it. And I'm tired of Taylor Motors being a joke. We have good people working in broken processes. We're going to fix our processes and will be asking many of you for help. Please support us."

J. Ed Morgan watched in silence with his arms crossed. This wasn't his project and I wasn't his boy. His grip on the company was slipping. Rachel, my patron, was his biggest threat. Fred May sat next to Morgan, smirking.

Around Morgan you feel like your fly is open. What's he think of a restaurant rat like me, or a steelworker's daughter like Rachel? Morgan had come of age in the 1960s. His hero was Robert McNamara, one of the "whiz kids" who came out of Harvard after WWII. Henry Ford II, aka Hank the Deuce, made McNamara president of Ford and asked him to fix the mess left by Henry the first. Then in 1960 John Kennedy asked McNamara to become Secretary of Defense.

McNamara and the whiz kids tried to transform management into a science, so they could manage "by hard numbers." I have no problem with that. It's necessary—but it's not enough. You can't motivate people by numbers alone. You have to engage the *heart*. I also know the "hard" numbers aren't so hard after all, and that standard cost accounting can be a lousy way to keep score.[7]

John Cafferty took some questions and then brought the meeting to a close. I shook hands with John and Rachel. Remembering my aikido training, I went over and shook hands with Morgan and May. Stay close to your enemies. Don't show the sword unless you have to. "We'll need your support, J. Ed."

"Indeed you will," said Morgan, sounding like William F. Buckley. May just looked at me, still smirking.

IMPLEMENTATION CHECKLIST

1. Deepen your understanding of reality by going to the gemba to see what's there.
2. Practice and teach Plan-Do-Check-Adjust to everyone in your organization.
3. Get close to your customers. Understand their explicit needs, and those they haven't articulated.
4. Respect your people. Involvement is the engine of improvement.
5. Develop simple, visual standards for all important things. Standardized work should comprise:
   - Content
   - Sequence
   - Timing
   - Expected outcomes

(continued)

---

[7] Real number accounting seeks to restore simplicity and clarity to financial statements and an organization's accounting system. For more information, please refer to *Real Numbers: Management Accounting in a Lean Organization*, by Jean Cunningham and Orest Fiume (Durham, NC: Managing Times Press, 2008), and to *Practical Lean Accounting*, by Brian Maskell and Bruce Baggaley (New York: Productivity Press, 2003).

(*continued*)

Standards should also contain embedded tests that tell you when there's a problem.

6. Foster a culture that makes problems visible, recognizing that problems are the system talking to us.

7. Practice exception management. Focus review meetings on Red (off-target) stuff, not Green (on-target) stuff.

8. Build quality into all your processes—by ensuring that your standardized work contains embedded tests. Don't ship junk. Get to the root cause and fix it.

9. Practice yokoten by sharing learning laterally, understanding that it's an antidote to Big Company Disease. Develop at least seven yokoten channels, with a bias toward face-to-face, experiential learning. Recognize that Google is necessary, but not sufficient.

10. Adjust compensation packages to reward leaders who build solid, sustainable management systems. Leaders must leave a positive footprint in the form of solid processes for manpower, machinery, methods, and materials.

11. Articulate your purpose in plain language and communicate it forcefully. Keep the main thing, the main thing. When it comes to purpose, it is impossible to overcommunicate.

STUDY QUESTIONS

1. Describe three mental models that exist in your workplace. Now draw them out using as few written words as possible. Drawing on the back of a napkin, by Dan Roam, provides insight into the power of visual thinking and tips on how to get started.

2. Describe current standards in your workplace.

   a. Are they simple, visual, and easy to understand?

   b. Who develops them?

   c. Do standards change? If so, describe the process.

   d. Check three standards in your workplace. Does work adhere to the standard? How do you know? If not, why not? How might you make it easier to check whether team members are following standards?

3. Assess visual management in your workplace.

   a. Is the current condition visible at a glance (e.g., customer requirements, ahead/behind, biggest problems, current countermeasures, process steps, bottlenecks)?

   b. If not, how might you improve it?

   c. What are the three corners of the visual management triangle? Is the visual management triangle satisfied in your workplace? If not, how might you improve?

4. How are problems viewed in your workplace—as gold to be treasured or as garbage to be buried?

   a. How might you change people's thinking about problems?

5. What is the stated role of leadership in your workplace?

   a. How do leaders actually behave?

   b. What do leaders reward and recognize?

6. Jidoka entails building quality into each process. Give three examples of jidoka in your workplace.

   a. How might you apply jidoka to improve three processes in your workplace?

Chapter 4   How Will We Change Their Thinking?

Our Town Hall kickoff generated a lot of blogging, almost all of it positive. People want us to succeed. Fred May's smirk bothered me though. Something bad was coming.

Regardless, I had to put my team together. I was looking for six people, each with a solid foundation in the basics:

- Value and waste
- Standardized work
- 5 S and visual management
- Flow
- Pull
- PDCA and problem solving
- Strategy deployment

I wanted both mavericks and system builders—people who could short-circuit the system and get things done, while building a better system! Antonio Villarreal and Rebecca Johnson, my NJMM team members, would anchor the team. They were both delighted to join us.

Antonio is stamping plant manager, a hip and creative Mexican who designs theater sets in his spare time. He understands both the people and the process side of Lean. Our stamping plant is world class. Moreover, Antonio has transformed our human resources activities, a special assignment I'd given him. He'll be our eyes on manufacturing and people processes.

"People make the difference," Andy taught us. Yet our human resource (HR) division is seen as Mordor, the realm of darkness. Maude Beecher, EVP of HR is widely reviled for her handling of our traumatic downsizing, during which veteran employees were treated like dirt.

Becky Johnson is a mechanical engineer from Fort Worth. She's a devout Christian who just returned from Peru where she helped to build an orphanage. Becky has helped transform our chaotic weld shop into an oasis of order and stability. Then I asked her to take on supplier development, where she also excelled. Becky will be our point person on the supply chain.

Andy and I chose four more team members from a list Bill Barrett had compiled: Sam Hendry, Kurt Schaeffer, Elaine Miyazaki, and Benny Walton. All were clever, tenacious, and impatient. My sense was that they were giving Taylor Motors one last chance.

Our first innovation was setting up an *obeya*, or "big room," an innovation pioneered by Toyota's Prius launch team. In fact, we set up two obeyas—one at CCM, where the vehicle would be built, and another in the Design Centre at Taylor City. Obeya's purpose is quick and effective communication to create a shared understanding and shorten the PDCA cycle. An *obeya* entails short focused stand-up meetings and simple visual management on the walls, including:

- Charts and graphs depicting program timing, milestones, and progress to date.
- Countermeasures to existing timing or technical problems.

Project leaders have desks in the obeya; others join us as appropriate based on program timing. We use the obeya to manage the schedule, identify hot spots, and create a daily, weekly, and monthly rhythm that hopefully would inform the entire platform.

I persuaded Anne Taylor, my fearsome NJMM assistant, to join the team as executive assistant. Managing information flow in the obeya would be a big part of her job. Our theme was Andy's elegant phrase, *neither too rigid, nor too loose.* Too much control and we'd stifle initiative and creativity. Too little control and people would get scared and tense up.

I called our first team meeting at CMM, where the vehicle would be built. Our objective was to develop an overall game plan. I began the session by describing all I'd learned during the past five years at NJMM. I described my dysfunctional mental models, how they'd held us back at NJMM, and how difficult it had been to change my thinking. I suggested that dysfunctional thinking was common among Taylor Motors' leaders, the product of years of conditioning. Then I posed Andy's troubling question.

"How will we change their thinking?"

Silence. It was a tough question, especially for a new team.

"Through direct experience," said Kurt Schaeffer finally. "You have to feel it in your gut."

Kurt is a manufacturing engineer from Aachen, Germany, and a graduate of that town's famous university. He has lived all over the world; his dad was a diplomat. Kurt speaks four languages, is a concert-level pianist, and moonlights in a jazz trio. He also apprenticed as a machinist and can shape metal as if it were clay. Kurt is a gentleman whose basic shyness makes him seem aloof, which has held him back in Taylor Motors' "appearance-is-everything" culture. He would be our window on vehicle engineering.

"Good answer, Kurt," I said. "So how do we provide visceral experiences for our management team? Remember that includes executives, functional managers, designers, engineers, and other specialists."

"Why don't we have Lean boot camps the way we do at NJMM?" Becky offered. "We could have sessions every quarter, each building on the last. We could invite 25 people or so and they'd get real problems to work on. Antonio, remember the changeover kaizen on Stamping Line 7?"

"It was a breakthrough," Antonio agreed. "The magic was in sharing the learning. Each team summarized their activities, and thinking, on one page, which went into our Book of Knowledge. Mr. Saito calls it *yokoten*."

"IT put everything on our intranet," Becky added. "Ya'll have seen it. It's pretty cool."

Andy was listening with his eyes closed. He opened them. "Internet is a good tool. But the most important learning is face-to-face. The deshi[1] must absorb the sensei's teaching and *apply* it in his own workplace. *Yokoten* means copy and *improve*."

"We've struggled with that at NJMM," I said. "Initially, we crowed about results rather than sharing and translating *thinking*. If you just copy, it doesn't work."

"Shared, lateral learning," Sam Hendry added, "is critical in design and engineering. I agree with Mr. Saito. Google is a great, but not sufficient for mastery. You can't learn rock climbing from the Net. You learn by *climbing* under the guidance of a veteran climber. You start small, with an indoor climb, say, and develop your skill and judgment. Each session builds on the last. In between you practice your technique."

Sam is a design engineer from Pasadena. He's an ardent rock climber and has scaled some of Yosemite's biggest "walls." His dad was a NASA engineer during the golden years, when NASA was putting people on the moon. Buzz Aldrin was Sam's inspiration, not only for his achievements as an astronaut, but also for his courage in confronting his alcoholism. "Buzz Aldrin is the real deal," I agreed. "Surprised you didn't go into aerospace." Sam laughed, "If this doesn't work out, I just might!" Sam is a contrarian, who moved to the east coast when everybody else was moving west. He would be our point man on vehicle design.

"Let me summarize," said Benny Walton. "We'll have quarterly learning sessions across the platform, led by our team. We'll adapt NJMM's teaching materials beginning with Lean basics like standardization and visual management. We'll work our way up to problem solving and other advanced stuff."

Benny is an African-American from Detroit who has been a star in supply chain, sales, and marketing. The latter was a developmental role and nobody expected much—marketing is a black box at Taylor Motors. But Benny beat the odds and made tangible improvements.

---

[1] *Deshi* means "student" in Japanese.

He grew up in Detroit's inner city and survived its scary public school system. Benny was a college chess champion and still plays high-level tournaments through the Internet. "Chess gave me clarity," he told me. "And it taught me how to focus for hours at a time." A pal of mine says that Benny is the hardest worker he's ever seen. He'll be our window on sales and marketing.

"Good idea, Benny," said Kurt. "We can run multiple sessions simultaneously, and grow a network of Lean thinkers."

"I like that," I said. "We want Lean leaders in each department, building their own network of Lean thinkers, and connecting it to our broader network."

Andy was pleased. "You are describing a Kaizen Promotion Office. A good way to developing thinking, but not well understood. We will need a yokoten strategy."

"Let's call it a Lean Coordinator Network," I offered. There was broad agreement.

"Normally, I'd ask that these be full-time assignments," I continued. "But I don't think we can swing it. I'll talk to Rachel about freeing people up at least part time for this work."

"What about executives?" Elaine Miyazaki asked. "They're responsible for *system* and *enterprise* kaizen—the most difficult of all. We need a parallel program for them."

Elaine is a business process analyst who has excelled in finance, marketing, and procurement. She's a third-generation Japanese-American; her grandparents had immigrated to America in the 1920s. Given her business process skills, she'd lead our activities in finance, human resources, and other administrative areas. I'd also ask her to help Bennie with the monster called dealers.

Elaine has a working knowledge of Japanese and Mandarin, and is a black belt in shotokan karate. When I asked Elaine about the "precepts" of shotokan, which Chiba-sensei had taught us at New York Aikikai,[2] Elaine rhymed them off. I recognized a warrior and bowed. She returned my bow, "Arigato gozeimas."

"Elaine's right," Sam offered. "But can we free up executives for three days a quarter?"

"We'll have to," I replied. "It's a test of their commitment."

---

[2] Tom's Manhattan aikido club.

Andy nodded. "Changing senior management's thinking is most important. Development programs must include *tests* that confirm learning and commitment."

The session went on like this. I was pleased. Here's a summary of our conclusions:

- For a successful launch we have to change *thinking* across the platform.
- To change thinking, we need to develop a network of Lean thinkers by providing quarterly, experiential learning sessions. Each session will:
  - Build on the previous session
  - Entail practical problem solving
- We will have parallel tracks for
  - Executives
  - Functional managers
  - Lean specialists, who would make up our Lean Coordinator Network
    - Per our request to Rachel, department heads would assign Lean coordinators to support the Chloe launch and Lean implementation.
    - Target ratio of one Lean coordinator per 300 people.
- Our developmental programs will include simple proficiency tests.

That weekend I had lunch with my brother Harry at the Humpty Dumpty. Harry told me about the latest breakthroughs in oncology, his specialty. "We're making incredible technical progress, but the overall system is as broken as ever."

"It worries me when dad goes to the hospital," I said. We worked out a game plan in case of emergency.

Uncle Angie sauntered in like the Sultan of Constantinople. He pulled up a chair. Big head, big gut, and curly gray hair; mama's younger brother—an entrepreneur, clarinet player, and raconteur. We exchanged pleasantries. Angie asked about my new job. "We have a good team," I said. "Lots of obstacles though."

"Be careful my boy. The whale that surfaces gets harpooned."

Angie then told us about his new business venture, a company called Roach Patrol.

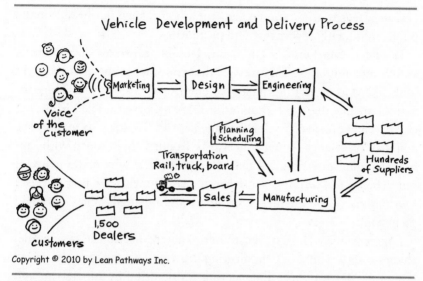

FIGURE 4.1　Vehicle Development and Delivery Process

"Wanna know the secret?" he asked.

Harry and I looked at one another. Angie put his hand over his mouth and leaned forward. "Don't kill them all."

Automotive engineering is a big deal; car guys and gals are a large and passionate group. I'm always impressed by their insights in John Cafferty's blogs. I planned to engage them in the Defiant's redesign.

The vehicle development and delivery process (Figure 4.1) comprises:

- Marketing
- Design
- Engineering
- Manufacturing
- Procurement (supply chain)
- Dealers

Marketing does research to understand the voice of the customer. This means focus groups, customer surveys, and the like. Marketing translates customer feedback into features and specifications. They also determine pricing and the communication strategy whereby the customer learns about our products. They also keep our brands in the public mind with advertising and promotion.

Design is Marketing's customer. Design translates customer research into miniature clay models that show what the vehicle might look like. Great styling makes an emotional connection. Think of iconic cars like the 1957 Thunderbird, 1958 Corvette, 1964 Mustang, or any car you love. Senior management in Taylor City makes the final call on styling—a big concern! Is Taylor City in touch with rapidly changing international markets? Moreover, why do so many of our vehicles *feel wrong*, even when the components are best in class? Our designers and engineers are smart and talented. What's holding them back?

Engineering is Design's customer. They translate the clay model shapes into detailed 3D engineering drawings using computer-aided design (CAD) software. Engineering is organized by subsystem, and by sub-subsystem, which we call modules. Engineering designs the subsystem and module, and the manufacturing process. *Integration* is the difference between a great car and an also-ran. Modules and subsystems have to fit together and be mutually supportive.

Manufacturing is Engineering's customer and has been my home for 20 years. Here's an extremely brief summary.[3] To make a vehicle, you have to *stamp it, weld it, paint it, and stuff it*. At NJMM we have about 2,000 team members and more than 500 manufacturing processes with cycle times in the 50 to 90 second range. We make 1,000 Desperados every day over two shifts.

Engineers in Taylor City design our manufacturing processes, which are usually lousy so that we have to redesign them in the plant. Luckily, we have a good relationship with our union and they allow us to make changes. Our contract says no changes 90 days after a product launch. In the bad old days we'd have been scuppered.

Our engineers are good kids but they're green. Because engineering is seen as dead-end, nobody puts in the time to develop profound knowledge. Nor do engineers ever come to the factory, which head office views as a backwater.

---

[3] For a detailed description of the auto manufacturing process, the interested reader is referred to *Andy & Me: Crisis and Transformation on the Lean Journey*, by yours truly.

So even though the Desperado is a cool car, it's hard to build. Our team members get ergonomic injuries from forcing ill-fitting wire harnesses, parts, and trim onto the chassis. Quality also suffers. To prevent water leaks, for example, we do a lot of sealing and resealing in our "hospital" at the end of Final Line.

Manufacturing's customer is sales, and ultimately, our 1,500 dealers. Are we aligned with our dealers? Each is an independent business usually run by a local entrepreneur. I rarely see dealers in our factory or at senior management meetings. As I mentioned, when I visit a dealer, it doesn't *feel* like Taylor Motors. And *every* dealer feels different.

Procurement manages our suppliers, which comprise up to 75 percent of our cost. We have hundreds, classified as Tier 1, 2, and 3. Tier 1 means they supply to us directly. These are also called Original Equipment Manufacturers (OEMs) and include companies that make our seats, tires, and other major components.

Are we aligned with our supply chain? Our VP of Purchasing, Joe Jacobsen, is a Fred May protégé and believes in sticking it to suppliers. For Jacobsen, as for May, piece price is all that matters. We'll replace a supplier for a shiny nickel—even if it imposes crushing costs downstream. We humiliate long-standing partners with reverse Internet auctions and the like. We dangle business like a carrot, and then yank it away at the last minute. One supplier exec was so upset, he grabbed Jacobsen by the tie and was going to deck him, before being restrained.

"We don't like working for Taylor Motors," a supplier told me. "Your procurement people are disrespectful. To be frank, we're after more Toyota, Honda, and Nissan business. They treat us as *partners*. Believe it or not, Toyota has expressed concern that our margins are not adequate. They've offered to *help* by sending the Lean team to work with us."

In spite of everything, during the past several years we've made some good moves in design and engineering. In particular, we've:

- Simplified our underlying platforms and architecture.
- Reorganized into 8 international Design centers and 10 Engineering centers, and tried to improve knowledge sharing between them.
- Focused global design centers on platforms they know best. North America now focuses on SUVs and trucks; Europe on compact cars, and Asia on subcompacts.

Over the next four weeks Andy and I visited every group that touched the Defiant. We asked questions and did a lot of listening. We did a gemba walk everywhere we went. I developed a list of questions that I put to team members in each area:

- Who is your customer?
- Who is your supplier?
- What's the process?
- What's today's work? What is this week's work?
- Are you ahead or behind?
- What are the biggest problems in your area?
- What are you doing about them?
- What are your strategic priorities this year?
- What are your corresponding action plans?
- How do you stand with respect to your strategic objective?

I drew many blank stares. For the most part, we saw cubicle farms with little visual management. In design I saw some wall charts and "war rooms" but the information was months out of date. I asked a young engineer manager about it. "A few years ago," he replied, "we colocated all our designers and tried to put all our data on the wall. But keeping it current was a hassle. We had endless report-out meetings. In fact, I stopped going to them. I don't need to know *everything*, only what affects my team and me."

At our Iron Horse debriefing, I summarized my observations to Andy. "Few people understand their objectives, current condition, processes, or customers. Most of the departments seem *dull*—there's nothing to see—and disconnected from customers and suppliers. Yet we've met many good people."

Andy took a pull on his bourbon. "Significance, Tom-san?"

I sampled my beer, a nice Irish lager. "These are knowledge workers. Their product is invisible—and waste is also invisible. If we make crap in the factory, everybody can see it. It we make crap in engineering, like a poor design or incomplete drawing—nobody can see it."

Andy nodded. "Can you define *value* in design and engineering, Tom-san?"

I'd been mulling it over. "Designers and engineers create value through knowledge."

"Any kind of knowledge?"

"*Usable* knowledge," I replied. "Value means creating usable knowledge. Everything else is waste—waiting for information, fixing incorrect drawings, looking for information, or sitting in unnecessary meetings. Oh, and too much information! That's overproduction. I remember that young engineer who said he *didn't want to know* everything—only what he needed to do his work."

Andy's eyes opened wider. "Correct, Tom-san! Now we begin to understand. Next question: Why did we see so little *kaizen*?"[4]

It was a good question—so many smart people, yet so few improvement activities. "Maybe knowledge workers are not conditioned to think about kaizen," I offered. "In the factory it's expected. At NJMM, we set improvement targets each year and deploy resources to help our team members get better at kaizen. You've taught us that '*kaizen is endless and eternal.*' Have designers and engineers been taught in this? Do they know how to make waste visible? Do they understand problem solving?"

It made sense. In business processes, waste is invisible and Lean thinking rare, which leads to a waste explosion. Nobody is immune. I told Andy about my cousin Danny's experience.

Danny recently ordered a Toyota Avalon. His local dealer relayed the order to Toyota North America, who in turn scheduled the work at Toyota's Kentucky factory. Danny got the car *28* days later. Dean Formica told me the car spends *less than two* days in the factory. So most of the lead time is outside the factory. And most of it is delay waste.

Andy agreed. "Toyota has had problems with its North American dealerships." Andy explained that Toyota had applied these hard lessons when they launched the Lexus brand 10 years ago.

I felt good about our team. We were beginning to grasp the situation. We had a plan on how to change thinking across the platform. We were ready to tackle the next question.

How do we focus and align our activities?

---

[4] *Kaizen* means "continuous incremental improvement" and requires the participation of everyone in the organization.

AUTOMOTIVE SYSTEM BASICS

Product and service delivery systems are complex nowadays. Not only are there many more silos, than say, 30 years ago, but the silos are much deeper and more specialized. To apply Lean thinking we need to do a systems analysis like the one that follows. You don't need to know this stuff to enjoy the book.

A *system* is an organized set of parts with a clearly defined purpose. A *vehicle* is a system whose purpose is to move us from point A to point B—in style and comfort. The parts or subsystems of a vehicle include the body, chassis, engine, fuel, lubrication, cooling, electrical, and transmission. There are also various mechanical subsystems including the axle, brakes, steering, and suspension. Then there are the various safety, security, and emissions control subsystems. Interior subsystems include the seats, heating and ventilation, stereo, and dashboard. See Figure 4.2.

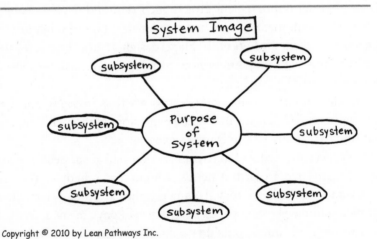

Copyright © 2010 by Lean Pathways Inc.

FIGURE 4.2 System Image

Each subsystem is a universe. Depending on how you count, a car is made of between 10,000 and 25,000 parts. I'm reminded of the Chinese puzzle boxes. As you unlock the secrets of one box, another is revealed, with its own set of secrets. See Figure 4.3.

Engines, for example, range in size from about 1.4 litres and up, and can have four, six, or eight cylinders. Engine power can be supplemented by turbo-chargers, super-chargers, and other power-boosting technology. Engines can be fueled by gasoline, diesel, or alternate fuels like ethanol, propane, or electricity, or hybrids of these.

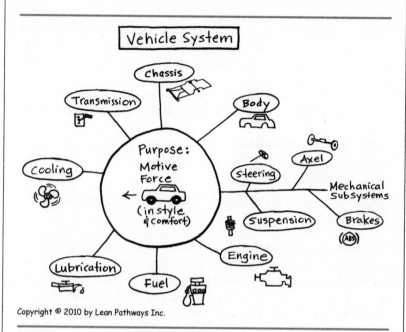

Copyright © 2010 by Lean Pathways Inc.

FIGURE 4.3   Vehicle System

The Defiant is a hybrid electrical vehicle (HEV) with a combination gas/electrical engine. HEVs have both an internal combustion engine (ICE) and an electric motor. Conventional ICE vehicles have a narrow speed and power "sweet spot"—in which they rarely operate. As a result, they're inefficient and emit higher levels of carbon compounds, nitrogen oxides, and particulates. By contrast, HEVs have a much wider sweet spot, which reduces gas consumption and pollution as follows:

- Less wasted energy during idling (by turning the ICE off).
- Waste energy is recaptured through "regenerative braking," which means converting the car's kinetic energy into electrical energy stored in its batteries.
- ICE can be smaller and less powerful.
- Electric motor compensates for the smaller ICE.

So HEVs are lighter, cleaner, and more efficient than conventional cars and can have just as much power. Taylor Motors missed the HEV boat a decade ago and is now playing catch-up.

(continued)

(continued)

Vehicle models are built on *platforms*. Originally, platform simply meant the chassis. But now it also means shared design, engineering, and production, and shared components. The physical platform comprises the following:

- Floor pan, the sheet metal stampings that form the foundation of the chassis.
- Wheelbase, the distance between the front and rear axles.
- Steering mechanism and type of steering.
- Type of front and rear suspensions.
- Placement and choice of engine, transmission, and other powertrain components.

Platform *architecture* is determined by how you lay these out. Typical questions include: What kind of engine and transmission do we want? Where do we put them? How long a wheelbase do we want? How much space do we allocate for our suspensions? A good platform strategy allows you to build multiple models on the same platform—which conveys great benefits:

- Flexibility—We're able to transfer production from one plant to another.
- Lower cost—We reap scale economies related to shared parts.
- Productivity—Because we can move production around we can keep our factories loaded.
- Speed to market and responsiveness—It's easier to design and make stuff, and to redesign it when tastes change.

Currently, the Defiant is the only platform that uses its particular hybrid architecture. If we're successful, we can use the same architecture for future hybrids, and for a sportier two-door Defiant coupe.

The danger of shared platforms is *homogeneity*. If everything looks the same, your lineup gets stale. You lose the customer's interest. Brands and models start to compete with one another. So our challenge is to build *distinct* models on shared architectures, reaping the benefits of sharing while meeting the needs of different customer segments around the world.

Platform architecture informs our design schedule, which comprises milestone dates at which subsystem designs are progressively frozen. Normally, chassis, body, and engine subsystem designs are frozen first. Designs for other subsystems typically stay fluid longer.

IMPLEMENTATION CHECKLIST

1. Set up shared space where you can make your current condition visible to all team members. Have regular stand-up meetings focusing on hot spots. If you are launching a major new product or service, consider setting up an obeya or "big room." Put critical real-time information on the walls. Create a shared understanding and shorten the PDCA cycle.

2. Develop a yokoten strategy for shared, experiential learning across your organization. Try to develop at least seven communication channels. Emphasize face-to-face, experiential learning. Recognize that yokoten is part of the remedy to Big Company Disease.

3. Develop a deep understanding of your business and current condition by going to see for yourself. Engage both the analytical and intuitive parts of your brain.

4. Do a systems analysis of your products, services, and processes. Recognize that grasping the situation is the prerequisite to meaningful problem solving.

5. Create ownership in your strategy by engaging others. Don't try to control things. Apply the river metaphor: Point the river to the sea, roughly define the river banks—and let it go.

6. Engage team members by asking questions. Apply Tom's insight: To suggest is to create. To define is to destroy.

STUDY QUESTIONS

1. How does *Yokoten* differ from "Best Practice Sharing?"
2. Define *value* in the following business process areas. Examples are included to help get you started:
   a. Marketing:
      - Value entails understanding customers' explicit and implicit needs and translating that understanding into specifications and features designers and engineers can use.
      - Other?
   b. Sales:
      - Value entails providing customers with information that helps them choose the best solution to their need or problem.
      - Other?

c. Design
- Value means translating marketing's customer insights into product and service designs that (a) can solve the customer's problem, and (b) engineering can translate into profitable value streams.
- Other?

d. Engineering
- Value means translating product and service designs into processes, and machinery that can profitably produce them at the customer's desired throughput rate.
- Other?

e. Finance
- Value entails providing financial information in simple, understandable forms so that we can make sound business decisions.
- Other?

f. Human Resources
- Value means developing people's skills and capabilities so that they can help solve the company's biggest problems and achieve its business objectives.
- Other?

g. Planning and Scheduling
- Value means creating production or service schedules that (a) reflect customer demand patterns, (b) are smoothed over time to minimize unnecessary variation for the production or service facility, and (c) are balanced across multiple facilities to maximize throughput at the least cost and effort.
- Other?

3. Give an example of each of the following kinds of waste in a software company. Examples are included to help get you started:

a. Motion
- Unnecessary reaching, twisting, and bending caused by poor workstation design (ergonomics).
- Other?

b. Waiting
- Waiting for instructions, designs, or other information from the upstream process.
- Other?

   c. Conveyance
- Delivering software in CD format to remote customers.
- Other?

   d. Correction
- Fixing faulty code
- Other?

   e. Overprocessing
- Multiple handoffs between designers caused by unclear specifications.
- Other?

   f. Overproduction
- Producing and delivering software earlier than the customer can use it.
- Other?

   g. Work in Process
- Too many projects in the hopper leading to long lead times and stressed programmers.
- Other?

   h. Knowledge
- Not tapping into the ideas and creativity of designers.
- Other?

4. Give an example of each of the following kinds of waste in a print advertising company:
   a. Motion
   b. Waiting
   c. Conveyance
   d. Correction
   e. Overprocessing
   f. Overproduction
   g. Work in Process
   h. Knowledge

Chapter 5 Focus and Alignment— When You're a Jet, You're a Jet

Strategy is storytelling. You have to answer two questions simply and clearly:

1. Where are we going?
2. How do we get there?

We're hardwired for storytelling. We engage the head and heart thereby our prehistoric ancestors gathered round the fire at day's end and spun tales. They didn't show PowerPoint slides.

Working with Andy has triggered in me a hunger for learning I thought I'd lost. I've learned that leadership is about *language*. Through words you create a vision that *pulls* people into the future. To create such a vision the leader has to be a philosopher. You have to reflect deeply on the following questions:

- Who are we?
- What do we believe in?

If you'd asked Eastman Kodak's people the first question 20 years ago, they might have answered, "We're a film company." If you asked them today, they'd likely answer, "We're an *imaging* company." Small change in words, vast change in opportunity.

If you ask Taylor Motors' people "who are you?" you'll get an array of answers: "We're a sales, marketing, finance, manufacturing . . . company." The range of answers reflects our misalignment.

The second question is rooted in *ethics*, the study of right and wrong. Peter Drucker taught us that a leader's job is to:

a. Get business results.
b. Create capability.
c. Reinforce core values.

I've come to understand that (b) and (c) are the means to achieving (a). We get results by growing people. People won't follow swine, at least not for long.

Answering the foundational questions gives us what Deming called *constancy of purpose*. The ancients called it *fortitude*, the strength of mind to endure suffering and adversity, and to never give up. Andy corroborated my thinking. "To be a good leader you must have a *big heart*." He made a gesture: a heart growing in his chest.

I thought about my ex-wife. I had defined Teal as a creep—the one who wouldn't let me see my children. Had I given her the benefit of the doubt? Had I been big-hearted with Teal?

Strategic planning at NJMM used to be a waste of time. At the beginning of each year, we'd spend days developing impressive PowerPoint "decks." The rest of the year we ignored them and desperately tried to "make the numbers." No reflection, no learning, no improvement.

Then Andy taught us *hoshin kanri*, the world's most powerful planning and execution system. We call it *strategy deployment* and it's become NJMM's brain and nervous system, making our "hot spots" visible, engaging all our people, and pulling Lean tools to where they were needed. Focus and alignment were the key to the kingdom. I would teach my team members the messy, human process we'd learned at NJMM.

Strategy deployment (SD) is "simple." Here are the basic steps:

1. Develop the plan.
2. Deploy the plan.
3. Monitor the plan.
4. Improve the system.

But there are many underlying layers of meaning. For example, we need to understand that there are two sides to managerial work:

1. *Routine work:* making the numbers.
2. *Improvement work:* improving the numbers—by improving the underlying system.

SD is about the *improvement* work. Where will we focus so we can escape the daily meat-wheel, the death spiral that crushes our spirit? I remember a poignant exit interview at NJMM, before we got better. Jeff was one of our most promising assistant managers but our daily chaos had broken him. "I don't mind taking crap if I do a bad job. But I don't even get a chance. I prepare my production schedule at 11:30 every night. By 7:00 AM it's shot to hell, and the spin cycle begins again. I take crap from everyone. I'm flyin' blind. Spend most of my time gathering info on yesterday's muck-ups: scrap, grievances, short shipments, breakdowns . . . I can't sleep. Got a hole in my stomach. I come in Saturdays and Sundays. My wife might leave me. Muck it—it ain't worth it."

I felt sorry for him. "What are you going to do?"

"I'm going into real estate."

We lost Jeff, and other fine team members, because we couldn't break the death spiral. All we knew was the desperate daily scramble to make the numbers—failing regularly, because the underlying system was broken. See Figure 5.1.

Years ago Stephen Covey[1] taught us that we need to invest in *important, nonurgent* work such as:

---

[1] *The Seven Habits of Highly Effective People*, by Stephen Covey (New York: Simon & Schuster, 2004).

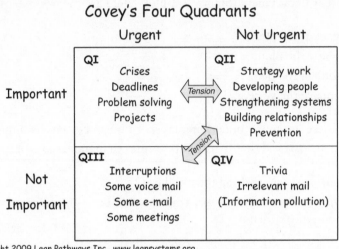

Copyright 2009 Lean Pathways Inc., www.leansystems.org

FIGURE 5.1   Covey's Four Quadrants

- Strategy
- Developing people
- Strengthening management systems
- Developing relationships
- Prevention
- Problem solving

Initially, we may only have a small window for such work, say, 5 percent of our time. But the more time we invest, the more time we free up; a benevolent cycle ensues. We begin to become Quadrant II leaders (see Figure 5.2).

Reversing the death spiral is hard to do. We become addicted to the adrenalin that accompanies chaos. Because nothing is stable people spend their time making things *look* good—by preparing fancy presentations, and ever more elaborate ways of solving the problem. Worst of all, the people who thrive in chaos naturally rise to positions of power—where they perpetuate the behavior that got them there. We reward arsonists. Notice that I *didn't* call them firefighters. Firefighters have standards, structure, and discipline—otherwise they die.

Chaos begets chaos. Weak companies tend to get weaker.

The QII Leader

QI	QII
	Strategy work
	Developing people
	Strengthening systems
	Building relationships
	Problem solving
	Prevention
	QIII & Q IV work

FIGURE 5.2   The Quadrant II Leader

We begin strategy deployment by defining True North, our strategic and philosophical goal. True North comprises both hard goals and a "broad-brush" goal or *hoshin*, which means a *brief expression on purpose, direction, commitment or values*. See Figure 5.3.

Hard goals speak to the head, and comprise "end-of-pipe" measures. For a major vehicle launch they'd comprise targets around Quality, Delivery, and Profitability:

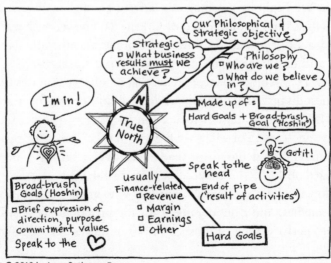

FIGURE 5.3   True North

Quality

• Defect per unit targets, process first time through; 3-, 6-, and 12-month in-service quality objectives met?

Delivery

• On-time launch? Production ramp-up schedule met?

Profitability

• Revenue, cost, and return on investment met?

Hoshins speak to the heart, by expressing who we are and what we believe in. Andy Saito's personal hoshin is: *Open Mind, Teamwork, Challenge!* I like Lexus' hoshin, *The Pursuit of Perfection*, coined by their renowned Shusa, Ichiro Suzuki. I also like Google's hoshin: *Do No Evil.*

Our hoshin at NJMM, *Take Action to Build Our Future*, informs all our activities. Each word has great meaning for us. Take Action! Build! Our Future! reflects our commitment to one another and to our community, and has helped create our "all for one and one for all" culture.

Once we've defined True North, we're ready for step 1: *Develop the plan.* We begin by grasping our current condition. *Where are we right now?* Is our condition Red or Green? To answer such questions we need good information flow and simple, visual tools like team boards and dashboards. Then we ask, *"What's preventing us from achieving True North?"* Sincere reflection on our weaknesses (hansei) and honest disagreement usually leads us to four or five focus areas.

At NJMM our strategy is focused in four areas: People, Quality, Delivery, and Cost. For each, we have a "mother A3" strategy and a "key thinker" or deployment leader. An A3 is simply a one-page storyboard on 11" × 17" paper.[2] See Figure 5.4.

Our key thinkers are "chief scientists" who grasp the situation, develop remedies, and gain alignment for the proposed actions. Breakthrough performance almost always requires cross-functional

---

[2] This template may be downloaded at www.leanpathwaysinc.com.

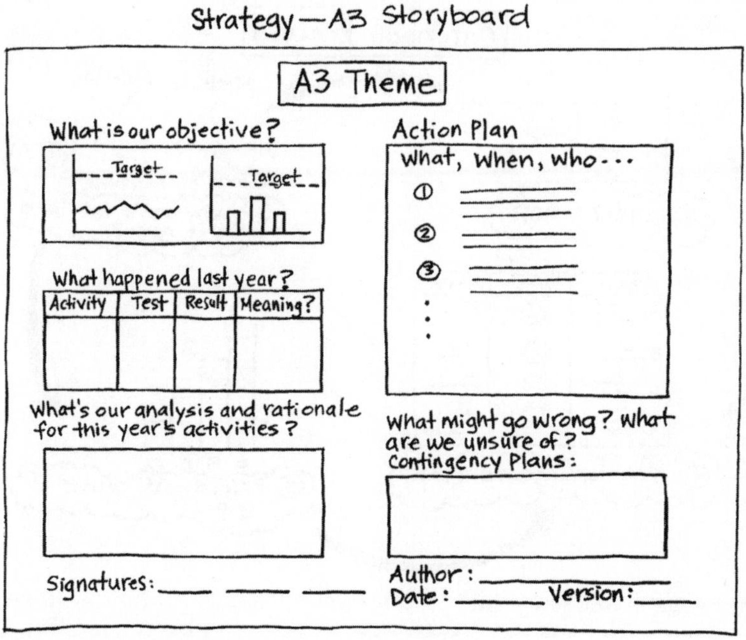

Strategy—A3 Storyboard

A3 Theme

What is our objective?

Target

Target

What happened last year?

Activity	Test	Result	Meaning?

What's our analysis and rationale for this year's activities?

Action Plan
What, When, who · · ·

① _____
② _____
③ _____
⋮

What might go wrong? what are we unsure of? Contingency Plans:

Signatures: _____

Author: _____
Date: _____ Version: ____

FIGURE 5.4   Strategy A3 Storyboard

alignment. Unit efficiency does *not* equal overall efficiency. A good team usually beats a collection of stars.

As key thinkers get stronger, their strategies get deeper and more robust. Each strategy is a hypothesis, a prediction of what will happen. Then we run the experiment, watch what happens, and adjust as required. It's a basic expression of the scientific method:

Thesis

• If I do this, I expect that will happen

Experiment and Observation

• What happened?

Synthesis

• Adjust hypothesis based on observed facts
• Keep going

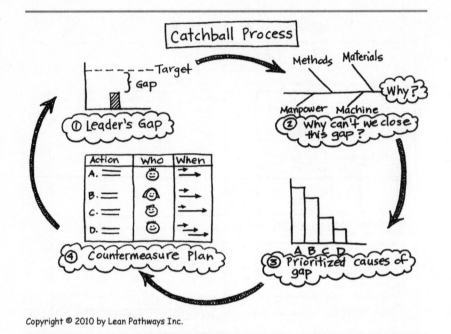

FIGURE 5.5   Catchball Process

Deploy the plan means translating our "mother A3" strategies into focused tactics in each business zone. The key word is *translation*. I've had my fill of Soviet-style planning: top-down, complex, confusing PowerPoint decks that alienate team members. We want zone leaders to ask, *"How can we best support the overall strategy?"* Done right, SD gives each team a small number of things to focus on.

The term *Catchball* reflects the give and take required to get to *what's real*. Catchball entails frank, fact-based discussions through which the leader's objectives are translated into meaningful tactics. Underlying these discussions is the process shown in Figure 5.5.

Catchball results in a tree of activities that connects the actions of each team member to True North. See Figure 5.6.

Metrics fall into two categories: *process* and *end-of-pipe* metrics. The latter represent your ultimate goals; the former, the *process* through which you will achieve them. In other words, $A + B + C = D$, where A, B, and C are the process metrics and D is the intended outcome.

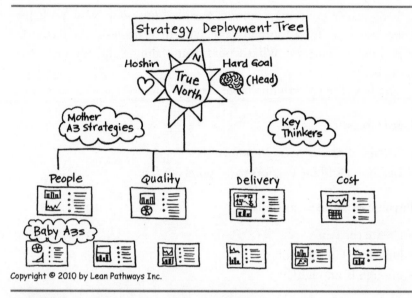

FIGURE 5.6   Strategy Deployment Tree

Catchball also helps to translate metrics. As we move down the tree, abstract, top-of-tree metrics like Margin or Return on Investment become concrete measures like minutes of delay, number of defects, and dollars of scrap. See Figure 5.7.

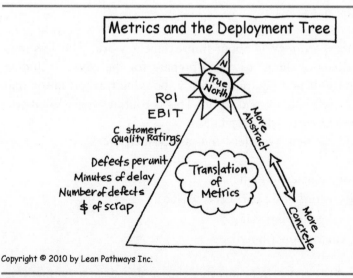

FIGURE 5.7   Metrics and the Deployment Tree

Let's take a concrete example. Suppose my poor New York Jets were preparing for a football game with their nemesis, the dastardly New England Patriots. What would their planning and execution tree look like?

The Jets' True North might be:

Hard Goals:

- Offense: Score at least 28 points.
- Defense: Hold the Patriots to 14 points or less.

Possible Broad-Brush Goals:

- Cream the Pats
- No More Humiliation
- Enough Is Enough!

The next level of the tree would comprise the Jets' tactics:

- Harass Tom Brady, the Patriots' brilliant quarterback.
- Control the ball and the clock with a good running game.
- No turnovers.
- Control the line of scrimmage.
- Perfect special teams.

Remember, strategy is about improvement work. The Jets may have hundreds of things to do to prepare for the game, including getting uniforms and equipment ready, booking transportation and hotels in New England, and so on. This is routine work. What will the Jets *emphasize* to win the game?

What are the New York Jets' end-of-pipe metrics?

- Score (for a particular game).
- Won-loss record (for a particular season).
- Did we make the playoffs?
- Did we win the Super Bowl?

Note that the end-of-pipe measure chosen depends on your *level of magnification*. If you zoom out to the entire season level, your metrics might be: Did we make the playoffs? Did we win the Super Bowl. The end-of-pipe measure for a given game, by contrast, is: Did we win the game?

Process metrics reflect our tactics:

Pressure on Brady

- Number of sacks
- Number of hurried passes

Control the Ball

- Running yards
- Time of possession

Turnovers

- Fumbles lost
- Interceptions

How might the Jets defense deploy the coaching staff's strategy? Here's a first cut at the Jets' planning and execution tree, showing how one subteam, Defense, might deploy the plan. See Figure 5.8.

I knew we'd have to apply the same process across our entire platform. Command and control failed in the Soviet empire, where they controlled all media, had secret police and gulags. How could it succeed at Taylor Motors in the age of Google?

We had more than 30 vehicle module teams. My small team and I would never know as much as each module team. We had to give the river direction, define the riverbanks, and let it run to the sea. But that doesn't mean we'd have no say in the path it took. In fact, the next SD element allows for a regular Check and Adjust of the river's path.

Monitor the system entails connected check meetings, and leaders "go see" activity, normally expressed in "leader standardized work." The latter refers to   activities you do every day, every week, and every month that provide your team with that crucial cadence or rhythm. Taken together these comprise a series of gears

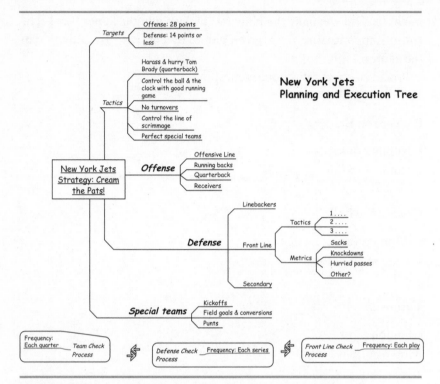

FIGURE 5.8   New York Jets Planning and Execution Tree

that connect frontline activity and the overall strategic direction. See Figure 5.9.

Gears are magic. A motive force in one part of a machine makes other parts move—at different frequencies! In a machine the gears are connected physically. In SD the gears are connected through information flow, good visual management, and shared mental models. If we accept, for example, that problems are gold, we'll make them visible at each level and problems will be the focus of our monitoring activities.

Here's a related mental model. Checking (see Figure 5.10) has a negative connotation in North America. *You're checking because you don't trust me.* Andy taught us that the purpose of checking is to:

- Show respect for the team's work.
- Reinforce the standard.
- Confirm a good condition.

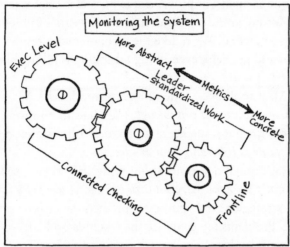

FIGURE 5.9   Monitoring the System

FIGURE 5.10   Purpose of Checking

Once our NJMM team got it, checking lost its sting.

Improving the system will be critical for the Defiant program. Improvement begins with *hansei*, Japanese for deep reflection and honesty about weaknesses. If you recognize your weaknesses with sincerity, a door opens; improvement is possible. My biggest concern is Taylor Motors' culture of denial. After 40 years of practice, we're the Masters of Denial. We're like the alcoholic who refuses to admit his problem and get help, even though drinking is killing him and his family.

At NJMM, it took us a while to understand hansei. We wanted to brag about our success. *Look at us!* Andy had to be severe with us. Kaizen's prerequisite is a sincere acceptance of mistakes and weaknesses. *My name is John and I am an alcoholic.*

Now we ask tough questions at our midyear and year-end strategy reviews: *What's broken? Why's it broken? How do we fix it?* We recognize our strategies are hypotheses, predictions of how our system will behave. Problems tell us where the system's broken. No big deal; something's always breaking. Now how do we fix it?

After several strategy deployment cycles, I detected a pattern. Our intended strategies usually morph into something . . . *better.* Our mother A3s are altered and improved through Catchball. Then they're fine-tuned further in our weekly check meetings. None of our plans go according to plan. But we usually achieve far more than we expected. See Figure 5.11.

I shared this with the team and asked what it meant.

Copyright © 2010 by Lean Pathways Inc.

FIGURE 5.11   What Actually Happens

"No plan goes according to plan," Antonio offered. "By defining where you're going and suggesting the means of achieving goals, you engage team members."

"By engaging team members," Elaine added, "you unlock their potential. Unexpected benefits follow."

Bingo. Strategy deployment was about helping people achieve their potential—as Taiichi Ohno had suggested all those years ago.

Andy concurred. "Hoshin kanri means unlocking team member potential. We cannot tell people what to do. This robs them of their responsibility to learn! By suggesting, we unlock organizational genius."

I mulled that one over: *organizational genius.* Taylor Motors had smart, dedicated people. How come we were so stupid an organization? What prevented smart people from expressing their knowledge and creativity? I would ponder these questions for a long time. In the interim, I wrote the following aphorism and image on a napkin. See Figure 5.12.

Andy then described his "river image." Strategy deployment entails defining direction and the outlines of the "riverbank." Then you

FIGURE 5.12   To Suggest Is to Create. To Define Is to Destroy.

have to let it go. Some water inevitably sloshes over the sides and you adjust through your check process. But you can't and shouldn't try to control it. The river inevitably gets to the sea.

Andy also talked about Sun Tsu, the ancient Chinese general, who likened strategy to aligning large boulders at the top of a hill. A good general knows where to position them for maximum effect. Then he lets them go. Our team members wrote furiously as he spoke. Then we were silent for a few moments.

"So how do we apply Strategy Deployment across our platform?" I asked.

"We start by defining True North," Kurt said. "We have to involve leaders from across the platform, and we'll need a deep understanding of customer value."

"Correct," said Andy. "The chief engineer and his team need to understand customer need in their guts. What is important to customers? What is not important? What makes customers happy—and unhappy? Please understand, market research, focus groups, competitive analysis is necessary. But it's not enough."

I had put my car into storage and now drove different Defiant models, in as many situations as I could conceive. I drove Sarah and the girls all over New York and Connecticut and listened carefully to their feedback. I talked to any Defiant owner who would speak to me, paying special attention to those who disliked the vehicle. I also drove competing vehicles and talked to *their* owners. In time I filled a thick notebook with observations. I wish I'd had more time. Andy told me about the Shusa who, seeking to understand customer need, had driven 50,000 miles, in every state of the Union, and province of Canada.

"We also need to connect with the Defiant platform leaders," Andy continued. "We need to show respect for their work and ideas. Normally, the Shusa will summarize thinking in a white paper. But we are too far into the process now."

Andy suggested a process he calls "Spew Out," whose purpose is to begin to answer our first strategic question: *Where are we going?* Our plan was to engage senior leaders in answering basic questions like:

- What do we call our vehicle?
- What does the customer *value*?

- How do we compare with our competitors: Prius, Insight, Fusion, and so forth—overall, and by component?
- How is our vehicle perceived in the market?
- How do we establish an emotional connection with the customer?
- What components do we need to redesign? What are the trade-offs?
- How do we improve our development system?

We scheduled a two-day session at the Design Centre in Taylor City and invited senior leaders from all groups that the touched vehicle, starting with marketing and ending with a sample of our dealers—about 30 people. Interest was high and everyone invited accepted our invitation.

Then Morgan and May tried to stab us in the back.

IMPLEMENTATION CHECKLIST

1. Reflect on the foundational questions:
   a. Who are we?
   b. What do we believe in?
2. Define True North, your strategic and philosophical objective, comprising:
   a. Hard goal(s), which appeal to the head.
   b. Broad-brush goal(s) or hoshins, which appeal to the heart.
3. Identify the biggest obstacles to achieving True North.
4. Develop one-page "mother A3" strategies for dealing with each obstacle.
5. Develop "Key Thinkers" to support the development and deployment of your mother strategies.
6. Translate mother strategies into meaningful targets and tactics throughout the organization through "Catchball."
7. Strengthen and standardize your check process at each level in the organization. Focus checking on out-of-standard items.
8. Teach all team members basic problem solving and free them up to attack the most important problems in their zone.
9. Reflect on what you've learned after each annual planning cycle. Share and record the learning.
10. Appeal to the heart, as well as the mind. Suggest a shared vision and let people fill in the details.

STUDY QUESTIONS

1. Describe your organization's management system. Is it clearly articulated? How is it communicated? How are team members trained in its elements? What is your organization's purpose (True North)?
   a. Hard goals
   b. Broad-brush goals (hoshins)
2. How is your organization's purpose communicated?
3. What are the end-of-pipe and process goals in your area?
4. Describe how objectives and plans are deployed in your organization.
   a. How might you improve deployment of objectives and plans in your organization?
5. Describe your organization's check process.
   a. How might you improve checking in your organization?
6. Is there meaningful reflection after each planning cycle?
   a. How effectively are learning points recorded, shared, and applied?
   b. How might you improve reflection after planning cycles in your organization?
7. Give at least one example of Tom's insight: To suggest is to create. To define is to destroy.

Chapter 6 Cluing into Chloe

"Given lagging Desperado sales and current economic conditions, we have no choice but to announce these layoffs at New Jersey Motor Manufacturing . . ."

I read the note on my BlackBerry with mounting anger. It would be released in a couple of days. Morgan and May would chop the entire second shift at NJMM—800 people. Weaker demand and our improved productivity gave them the excuse they needed. It would shatter morale and make a liar out of me. I had promised that nobody would lose his or her job because of kaizen.

I called Rachel. Turns out she had been fighting a rearguard action for some time. Rachel was furious with Maude Beecher, our EVP of Human Resources, who had sided with Finance. "You'd think an HR VP would look after people."

With Beecher on his side, Morgan went to Cafferty and asked him to sign off on the layoff. Cafferty had agreed "with regret." Great leadership, John, I thought.

Andy frowned when I told him. We had just finished our daily walk-through at CMM and were heading to the obeya. "The cost saving is false," he said. "Volume will recover, but morale will not."

"It's bizarre," I said. "Why would they sabotage us? The company *needs* a successful launch. We've just come out of bankruptcy."

"Very strange," Andy agreed.

I took a deep breath. "I won't accept it."

Andy and I got coffee out of the vending machine, went to a whiteboard and did some brainstorming. Half an hour later, we had our plan. It was bold and a little crazy. I called Rachel and told her. She was silent for a moment. "In the circumstances, I understand. I'll have Brenda set up a teleconference with Fred May."

Brenda called me back 10 minutes later. Fred May and Rachel were on the line. I put them on speakerphone. "Hi Fred, Tom Papas here with Andy Saito. I just got the memo."

"It's too bad," May replied, "but we really had no choice. Unfortunately, cost walks on two legs."

"I'm afraid I don't have a choice either, Fred. I've just given Rachel my notice of resignation. *I quit.*"

"What do you mean you quit?" May exclaimed. "It's the worst recession since the 1930s. You can't quit."

"Mr. Saito and I are starting a Lean consultancy," I went on. "I made a commitment to NJMM team members. This layoff is a betrayal of that trust."

"We cannot continue under such circumstances," Andy added. "There is much opportunity in consulting. We will begin with Toyota suppliers."

May was silent. This wasn't going the way he'd planned.

"I'm going to call John Cafferty now," Rachel said. "The press will have a field day. One of our top manufacturing guys agrees to lead the Defiant platform. A month later he quits to work with Toyota suppliers. I'm also going to call Art Juna. He won't be happy."

"Hold on here," May interjected. "The memo's just a trial balloon. Let me talk to J. Ed Morgan. The final decision hasn't been made."

"We need an answer tomorrow," said Rachel.

With that, Andy and I headed for dinner at a nearby sushi restaurant. We talked to Rachel on my BlackBerry while sipping sake. "It's a worthwhile gambit," she said. "I'd hate to lose you, Tom. But if

Morgan and May get away with this, the game is up. Hell, I might be joining your consultancy! It bugs me that Maude Beecher went to the dark side so readily."

"Sounds like we've got another enemy," I said.

"I think you're right, Tom," Rachel replied. "But we have an even more powerful ally. Art Juna gave Morgan and May a public dressing down at the last board meeting. Told them that bean counters were responsible for Taylor Motors' collapse, and he'd be damned if he'd let them do it again. Taylor Motors would focus on making great cars—and Finance better get with the program. Quite a performance."

I laughed. "I'd have paid to see that!"

"Juna's making a series of TV commercials. Wait'll you see them— he's a natural!"

Andy and I enjoyed an oddly calm and pleasant dinner. I had been with Taylor Motors my entire career and was about to walk away. Part of me was looking forward to consulting with Andy. He suggested we consider working outside of manufacturing. "There is much need in health care, financial services, and other areas." It sounded pretty good—health-care work, in particular—given my dad's experience.

But the next day Fred May sent us a fawning note. "We've been able to find efficiencies elsewhere in the system, which makes the proposed closing unnecessary. Thanks for working with us on this. . . ."

You weasel, I thought. We'd lived to fight another day, but I was sick of playing defense, sick of worrying about Finance goons. Art Juna had inspired me. No more defensiveness. I would take the battle to them. From now on I'd be kicking ass and taking names.

But something didn't make sense. Why would Morgan and May try to sabotage us? Our failure could well hasten the company's failure. Was it a high stakes game of chicken—or was something else afoot?

The following week we held a two-day Spew Out session with platform leaders in our Design Centre obeya. Almost all the senior managers and directors who touched our platform attended and sat at round tables in groups of five or six. It was the first time I'd met many of them. Andy Saito and all my team members also attended; the latter would serve as table captains. Thanks to Rachel, I had the undivided attention of attendees. A big part of their bonuses would depend on how well we worked together.

I felt wholly inadequate as I stood up front preparing to kick off the meeting. *What do I know about anything?* My years fronting an R&B band helped—I knew how to belt it out, even if it wasn't very good.

Andy found my discomfort amusing. "Remember, Tom-san. In the kingdom of the blind, the one-eyed man is king!"

"Yeah, but I'm one of the blind," I whispered back.

"Mr. Saito and I have spent the past six weeks walking our vehicle development process," I began. "It's clear to us that Taylor Motors is suffering from Big Company Disease. We have smart, talented people working in broken processes, which prevent them from expressing their knowledge and creativity. We develop vehicles *in spite* of our management system—not because of it."

I looked around the room. Body language was a bit stiff; facial language noncommittal. "Our purpose—you and I—is not only to launch a great vehicle. It's to develop a *remedy* for Big Company Disease. Our deliverable will be a better development process, a system that we can teach the rest of the company. We don't want bureaucracy—it doesn't work. We want a system that's neither too rigid, nor too loose. It'll mean fewer signatures for approval, less paperwork, and more collaboration. We'll be asking each of you and your teams to contribute. As I said in our Town Hall session, I'm tired of losing. And I'll bet you are, too.

"Part of the remedy is changing our basic thinking. In the months to come my team and I are going to invite you and your team members to practical training sessions in the principles of Lean management. We want to grow a network of Lean thinkers across our platform. We'll also ask your Lean thinkers to replicate the teaching in your zones. My team will provide guidance, training materials, and expertise. We'll serve as the hub of our network, if you will. But we do not intend to control it. You can't control learning."

I went on like this for another minute or so. They looked skeptical. Then I described the purpose of our session:

- To provide an overview of Strategy Deployment, our compass.
- To answer the following questions:

- *What does our customer value?*
- *What's True North?*
  - Hard goals
  - Broad-brush goal (hoshin)
- What's preventing us from getting there?
- To begin to develop trust and camaraderie.

I then introduced Andy who gave a brief overview of the *Spew Out* process and concluded with, "Tonight we are having a group dinner. No spew out please!"

Here's our two-day agenda:

Day One

8:00 to 9:30 AM Overview of Strategy Deployment—Antonio, Becky

9:30 to 10:30 Marketing Perspective—Marketing Director

Where is the HEV market going?
How do we compare with the competition?
How is our vehicle perceived in the market?

10:30 to 10:45 Break

10:45 to 12:00 What are our Strengths, Weaknesses, Opportunities, and Threats?

12:00 to 1:00 PM Working Lunch

Overview of Design Considerations—Design Director

1:00 to 2:30 Waste Walk and Report Out

2:30 to 3:30 Where is HEV technology going?—Engineering Director

3:30 to 4:30 Overview of Procurement Status—Supply Chain Director

4:30 to 5:00 Reflection, feedback, and homework in preparation for day two

Day Two

8:00 to 9:00 AM Review of feedback from day one. Teach Lean basics

9:00 to 10:30 Visual Management Walk and Report Out
10:30 to 12:00 Team Breakouts
What's True North?
12:00 to 2:00 PM Working Lunch
What's Preventing Us from Achieving True North?
2:00 to 4:00 Team Breakouts
Where Do We Focus Our Activities?
4:00 to 4:30 Reflection, feedback, and next steps

We used our time together to teach some Lean basics. On day one we spent an hour in the gemba doing a Waste Walk.[1] On day two we did a visual management walk. These entailed small groups walking through a designated area (e.g., a design office, prototype shop) and recording what they observed—and what it meant. They then prepared a short presentation of problems observed and possible countermeasures. Our rationale was: People learn by doing.

We implemented a small group activity we called *teach back*, where people prepared a short lesson on an important concept using images only. Each teach back comprised no more than four minutes, at which point the presenter received a Red card—Stop. At three minutes they got a Yellow card. We wanted to encourage a consciousness and respect for time—the one resource we cannot rent, lease, or buy. Delay waste was the killer in new model launches—we were determined to make it visible.

We also introduced the Plan-Do-Check-Adjust (PDCA) cycle by asking for feedback at the end of each day:

- What are three things you learned today?
- What are three things you didn't learn?
- What can we do to improve?

Small things, I know. But I'd learned that culture is made up of such small things. I'd also learned that you are what you do.

Antonio and Becky began the session with an overview of Strategy Deployment, which they illustrated with NJMM stories. I emphasized

---

[1] Waste Walk and Visual Management Walk templates are downloadable at www.leanpathwaysinc.com.

the idea that strategy was storytelling and gave attendees a list of relevant books. "We all have to go 'back to school,'" I told them. Nobody argued.

Marketing, Design, Engineering, and Supply Chain leaders then provided overviews of their zones and insights into where our market segment was heading. I had asked them to avoid PowerPoint junk and to boil things down to one page where possible. I was pleased with the depth and clarity of their presentations. We had good people indeed.

Many directors had never met before. Design is a people process that depends on a web of informal connections—connections built on trust and respect. You make those connections by breaking bread, sharing difficulties, and solving problems for one another. But the Taylor Motors launch process didn't foster such connections. Good people in broken processes.

Breakout sessions began awkwardly. Andy asked each group to illustrate their thinking through *images*. Silence. *You want us to draw?* But the atmosphere changed. People found that drawing out their ideas was fun and effective. Soon the conference room was full of laughter and loud, happy voices.

The definition of hard goals was fairly straightforward and comprised high-level end-of-pipe objectives for Profitability, Quality, and Delivery:

- Profitability
  - Return on investment
  - Annual revenue
- Quality
  - In-use quality (3, 6, and 12 months in service)
  - J.D. Power Customer Satisfaction Index
- Delivery
  - On-time launch
  - Time to volume
  - Overall lead time (customer order to delivery)

I explained we would deploy a tree of objectives and activities across our platform. Each department would translate high-level goals into objectives that made sense in their zone. Then, they'd figure

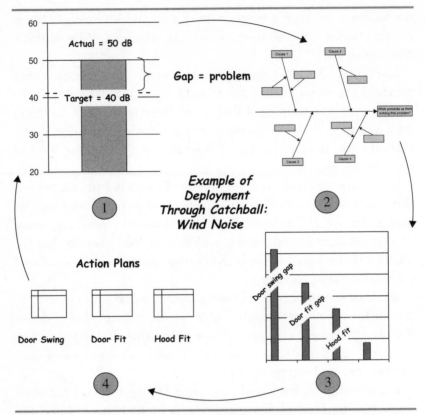

FIGURE 6.1   Example of Deployment Through Catchball

out activities to meet their objectives. I used my New York Jets example to illustrate. Lightbulbs began flickering. See Figure 5.8.

Andy then took the group through an automotive example, showing how, through Catchball, we could translate a high-level wind noise objective into focused objectives for module teams. More lightbulbs. See Figure 6.1.

The output was a planning tree of metrics similar to the New York Jets tree. See Figure 6.2.

Andy explained that the subteams would translate their gaps into action plans in exactly the same way. This was the essence of Catchball—scrubbing away until we get to *what's real*. The group absorbed it in silence. Finally, the engineering director piped up. "That just makes so much sense. Why do we complicate things?"

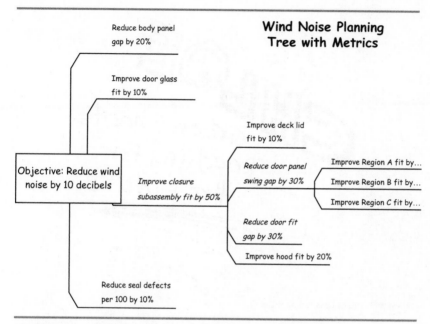

FIGURE 6.2   Wind Noise Planning Tree with Metrics

The broad-brush goal presentations were loud and intense. Long-repressed frustration came to the surface. Turns out few people liked the name *Defiant*. "Guess who picked that name?" a marketing leader exclaimed. "Not marketing! Our choice was overturned by, wait for it, *Finance*. Got that? Some bozo in Finance chose the name. They also tried to control our entire marketing and communications strategy! Sorry, I'm getting upset here."

After raucous and often angry debate, the group agreed on the following name and hoshin for our vehicle (see Figure 6.3):

Chloe means "green shoot" in Greek, and is another name for Demeter, the ancient Greek goddess of the earth. It felt right to me, but what did I know about marketing? Our marketing director liked it, too, but said she wanted to confirm it through concept and brand testing. She also wanted to do some "cool-hunting." I nodded—clueless. Another reminder about how much I had to learn.

The teams also provided useful insights into what the customer valued. Again, we boiled things down to their essence. Here are some key words:

Copyright © 2010 by Lean Pathways Inc.

FIGURE 6.3 Chloe—Green Shoots Reaching for the Future

- Stylish
- Reliable
- Great mileage
- Styling makes a statement
- Want to feel good about my purchase
- Want people to notice it

There was likely some vanity here—*Look at me! I'm environmentally conscious.* But our job was to delight customers, not to question them. Here are the main things our customers do *not* like:

- Styling—does not make a statement
- The interior feels cramped
- Wind noise
- Squeaks and rattles
- Seats too low
- Inadequate lumbar support
- Dashboard—some of the plastic looks cheap

- Black mirrors look cheap
- Doesn't handle as well in snow as heavier vehicles

These assessments also felt right and were in line with my initial impressions of the vehicle. But again, I felt self-conscious. Were these the right things to focus on? What did I know about what the customer valued? Had I truly grasped the situation?

Nonetheless, the team seemed happy and energized. There was broad agreement that we could translate these into a focused list of innovation projects. The engineering director was relieved. "I was afraid we'd need to start from scratch. But we can handle these innovations. Styling will be our biggest challenge. We want a few tweaks to make it eye-catching—without triggering major die redesign!"

"I'd like to be involved in die design," Antonio offered. "I can share what we learned at NJMM. I'll bet we can apply them in our prototype shops."

"Happy for the help," the engineering director replied.

I was pleased. Fabrication and testing of prototypes is a big part of design. Die design delays were a major cause of the late Defiant launch. Yokoten was beginning.

We had defined True North. Now we had to define the next level of the tree, which would determine where we focused our activities. The New York Jets are a relatively small organization and could go directly to functional action plans. In other words, the defensive and offensive coordinators could directly translate the Jets' overall strategy into tactics.

But we were a much bigger and more complex organization. Thus, we needed an intermediate level in our tree that would provide corresponding direction to the tacticians in each zone. This was the second level of our tree. We began by asking, *what's preventing us from achieving True North?*

Each group used a common brainstorming tool called an Affinity Chart. The process is simple:

- Each group member writes down everything he can think of on sticky notes and sticks them on the wall.
- Once the wall is full, the team organizes the sticky notes around common themes.

- Ground rules:
  - Each person comes up with at least seven ideas.
  - There are no bad ideas.
  - We go for volume and filter later.

This exercise also generated strong debate. Here is one group's affinity chart—after they grouped ideas into common themes. See Figure 6.5.

Now I proposed that we translate the top-level groupings into the following focus areas and that my team members act as Key Thinkers:

We're Misaligned with the Customer—*Profitability*

- Key Thinker: *Benny Walton*

Design, Engineering, Manufacturing, and Procurement Are Misaligned—*Delivery*

- Key Thinker: *Sam Hendry*

Quality Is an Afterthought—*Quality*

- Key Thinker: *Kurt Schaeffer*

We Don't Develop People—*People*

- Key Thinker: *Elaine Miyazaki*

Weak Management System—*Management System*

- Key Thinker: *Antonio Villarreal*

Becky Johnson would be our Key Thinker for our planning and execution system, a critical role I'd learned to appreciate in our NJMM deployment.

The Key Thinker's immediate job would be to define second-level hoshins, short action phrases that would give direction to the functional teams. I made up the following sample *People* hoshins to show what things might look like:

What's Preventing Us? (Organized)

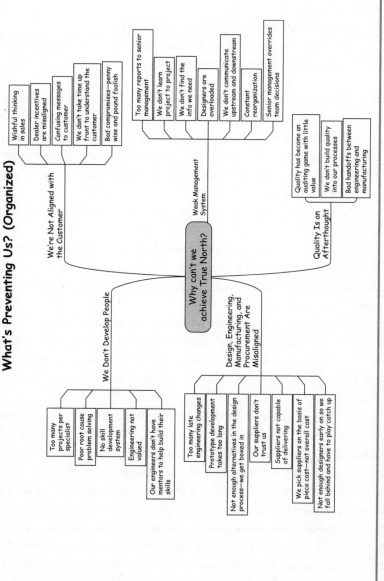

We're Not Aligned with the Customer
- Wishful thinking in sales
- Dealer incentives are misaligned
- Confusing messages to customer
- We don't take time up front to understand the customer
- Bad compromises—penny wise and pound foolish

Weak Management System
- Too many reports to senior management
- We don't learn project to project
- We don't find the info we need
- Designers are overloaded
- We don't communicate upstream and downstream
- Constant reorganization
- Senior management overrides team decisions

We Don't Develop People
- Too many projects per specialist
- Poor root cause problem solving
- No skill development system
- Engineering not valued
- Our engineers don't have mentors to help build their skills

Design, Engineering, Manufacturing, and Procurement Are Misaligned
- Too many late engineering changes
- Prototype development takes too long
- Not enough alternatives in the design process—we get boxed in
- Our suppliers don't trust us
- Suppliers not capable of delivering
- We pick suppliers on the basis of piece cost—not overall cost
- Not enough designers early on so we fall behind and have to play catch up

Quality Is an Afterthought
- Quality has become an auditing game with little value
- We don't build quality into our processes
- Bad handoffs between engineering and manufacturing

Why can't we achieve True North?

FIGURE 6.5   What's Preventing Us? (Organized)

- Develop practical Lean learning process based on learn-by-doing for platform managers and specialists.
- Develop yokoten (experiential learning) program for designers and engineers.
- Confirm and enrich technical career pathways.
- Develop user-friendly lessons learned process so we don't have to solve same problem over and over.

The group began to understand what "neither too rigid, nor too loose" meant. We had agreed on overall objectives and direction. But our platform leaders would have to translate these into meaningful tactics in their zone of control. And they'd have ample opportunity for feedback. They also knew we'd be having regular Check/Adjust sessions in our obeya.

To see how our planning and execution tree looked, take a look at Figure 6.6.

That evening we had a group dinner that continued the slow process of building trust and camaraderie. Body language was more open and relaxed. There were jokes, toasts, and a growing sense of optimism. *This could work!*

Day two was just as productive. By day's end we had met all our objectives and the conference room was aglow. Andy thanked everyone for a "good spew out." "Chloe is officially born," I told them. "Let's give her a soul." Then I asked for reflections and final comments.

John Winter, a silver-haired Alabaman and respected design executive stood up. "Tom, I want to thank you, Mr. Saito, and your team for one of the best kickoffs I've ever attended. I appreciate your openness, commitment, and common sense. We got more accomplished in two days than I thought possible. I learned a great deal and made new friends. I think we all did. I'm looking forward to working with ya'll."

"That means a lot to me, John," I told him. Andy bowed. "You are very kind, John-san." I thanked everybody for coming, announced the date of our next session, and brought the meeting to a close. The session ended with handshakes, bear hugs, and laughter.

That night, we had a surprisingly good sushi dinner at Detroit Metro Airport. The team was aglow and relieved at having passed an important test. I was relieved, too. My doubts had begun to subside.

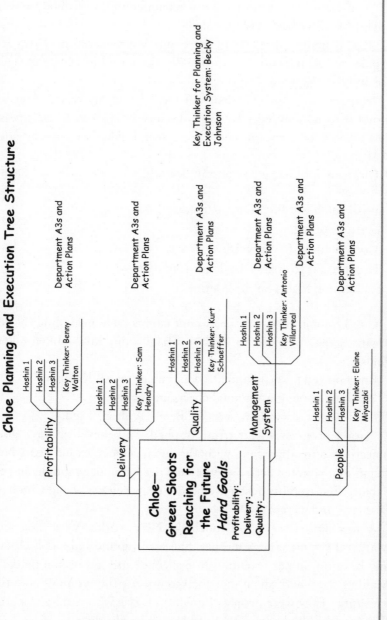

Chloe Planning and Execution Tree Structure

Chloe—
Green Shoots
Reaching for
the Future
Hard Goals
Profitability: _____
Delivery: _____
Quality: _____

Profitability
- Hoshin 1
- Hoshin 2
- Hoshin 3
- Key Thinker: Benny Walton

Department A3s and Action Plans

Delivery
- Hoshin 1
- Hoshin 2
- Hoshin 3
- Key Thinker: Sam Hendry

Department A3s and Action Plans

Quality
- Hoshin 1
- Hoshin 2
- Hoshin 3
- Key Thinker: Kurt Schaeffer

Department A3s and Action Plans

Management System
- Hoshin 1
- Hoshin 2
- Hoshin 3
- Key Thinker: Antonio Villarreal

Department A3s and Action Plans

Department A3s and Action Plans

People
- Hoshin 1
- Hoshin 2
- Hoshin 3
- Key Thinker: Elaine Miyazaki

Department A3s and Action Plans

Key Thinker for Planning and Execution System: Becky Johnson

FIGURE 6.6 Chloe Planning and Execution Tree Structure

If I applied Lean fundamentals and worked hard, maybe I could be a chief engineer.

"You came across well," Kurt Schaeffer said. "Nobody else at Taylor Motors could play the role."

"It's the undiscovered country," Elaine Miyazaki put in. "Very few people can *see* the entire platform—let alone lead it. Most managers are down in the weeds."

"I appreciate your confidence in me," I told my team "And I'm proud of you. You led your table discussions with skill and finesse. You asked good questions and made it real. I didn't see any arrogance or rigidity."

Our team internalized important lessons:

- Small batch learning. *Drip, drip, drip* . . .
- Learn by doing.
- More pictures, fewer words.
- To suggest is to create. To define is to destroy.
- Each lesson builds on the last one.

Good timing, too—our Lean boot camps were beginning the following week. I turned to Andy. "Thank you, Saito-san, for your guidance."

Andy bowed his head and lifted his cup of sake. "Kampai."

We drained our glasses amid cheers and grins.

"Any words of wisdom, sensei?" Benny Walton asked.

"Good progress so far, Andy replied. "I believe we have good objectives and alignment with the management team. Lean boot camps and yokoten activities will help deepen understanding and capability. But to move faster we need a deeper grasp of Big Company Disease—and its remedy."

A few days later I had lunch on New York's West side with Margaret Orcutt, Teal's mother. She was a grand lady, still elegant and beautiful in her seventies. In her youth she had been a model in Manhattan, where she'd met Joe Orcutt, a rising young marketing executive. They were people of grace and style who had lived a great life together. I had hoped Teal and I could be like them.

"I was so pleased to get your invitation, Tom," she said. "Joe and I have missed you."

"I've missed you, too," I replied. "Hope you don't hate me . . ."

"Tom, we could never hate you. You've given us two beautiful granddaughters, and were always a good son-in-law. It takes two to tango, sweetheart. I know how difficult Teal can be."

"That's what I wanted to talk to you about. I don't want to fight with her anymore. I want a good relationship. We've caused one another enough pain."

Margaret looked at me. "Yes, you have."

"Would Teal be open to a better relationship?"

"I think she would be. You know, Tom, your relationship with Sarah has been hard on Teal. Not that she wants you back. I think she realizes a relationship involving two alphas doesn't work. But it's been hard on her."

I felt compassion for my ex-wife.

"You may not know this," Margaret went on, "but Teal is *proud* of you. She always says, 'Look where he started, and look at him now!'"

I'd like to be Teal's friend, "Margaret. I'd like us to work together."

"You call her," said my ex-mother-in-law.

IMPLEMENTATION CHECKLIST

1. Engage your management team in defining True North, your strategic and philosophical objective.

2. Use Spew Out sessions to understand value from the customer's point of view. Recognize that "customers" can be internal, as well as, external.

3. Identify the biggest obstacles to achieving True North.

4. Develop one-page "mother A3" strategies for dealing with each obstacle.

5. Translate mother strategies into meaningful targets and tactics throughout the organization through "Catchball."

6. Focus on the critical few—at each level.

STUDY QUESTIONS

1. When Tom Papas learns of the planned layoff at NJMM, he offers his resignation.
   a. What is integrity and how does it relate to standards?
   b. Is integrity possible in the absence of standards? Explain your answer.
   c. Describe a work situation where your integrity was challenged. How did you react? What did you learn?
   d. Why is integrity important for leaders?
   e. How does this relate to Strategy Deployment?
2. Describe your organization's process for understanding value from the customer's point of view?
   a. How might you improve this process?
3. How does your organization determine and deploy design objectives?
   a. How might you improve the current process?
4. How does your organization disseminate learning?
   a. How might you improve the current process?

Chapter 7 A Trip to Boston to Dispel the Fog

Another day, another plane ride. The Boeing 727 rose above Queens and Manhattan and headed north toward Boston. Andy and I were visiting a couple of electronics suppliers to assess their capability, and their openness to joint kaizen. Chloe needed suppliers who were not only capable, but also cooperative. It would be an uphill battle, given how we've treated them.

Andy suggested we also drop in on Dr. Sam Sparrow, a management studies professor at Boston Institute of Technology (BIT). Sparrow had worked with Andy a decade ago as part of his doctorate. I was surprised. Like most plant managers, I'm impatient with academics—shiny-asses, Bill Barrett called them. What had this fellow done to warrant Andy's attention?

Andy was taking a snooze. I sipped tomato juice and looked out the airplane window. The rising sun seemed to mirror my hopes. The financial tsunami was receding. The economy was showing signs of life and we started selling cars again. Our new models, including Chloe, were generating a positive buzz. We were the underdog now and many people were rooting for us. I knew others saw us as corporate welfare bums.

We were four months into our journey and eight months from the Chloe launch. Our first round of Lean boot camps had been a success—both the executive and Lean coordinator streams. Most executives were open and honest. They seemed to realize this might be our last chance. Might as well tell the truth.

We had a few jackasses. Executives who knew everything and who believed waste walks and basic problem solving were beneath them. Two British bozos, in particular, gave Antonio and Becky a hard time. They wanted to do everything at once—because Lean was so easy. Their body language was transparent. *This is a crock. If people would just do as I say. . . .*

Executive arrogance could be a major obstacle, I realized. In the absence of cross-functional alignment through strategy deployment and the Shusa, large companies easily degenerated into warring city-states. And as in the Italian renaissance, this made them easy pickings for predators. Without Rachel and Art Juna, cement-heads could well have shut us down. The financial crisis had opened a window. Taylor Motors was getting some fresh air.

Our Lean Coordinator Network had formed its first links. For the most part, division leaders had staffed these positions with talented people. Chloe's strategy had been reasonably well deployed; the consensus was that the platform was better focused and aligned. Now we would launch a series of carefully considered kaizens in each zone—starting way upstream in marketing and cascading all the way downstream to our dealer network.

Initially, we got pushback on boot camp content. "This is too basic. We want to learn advanced stuff. . . ." But we persisted, knowing our managers didn't really understand waste, standards, visual management, and other fundamentals.

We emphasized thinking, instead of tools, and provided simple handouts, instead of thick glossy binders. Our curriculum included practical tests and report outs, where people drew out responses to difficult questions. We rarely gave answers. Andy had taught us that doing so took away "the student's responsibility to learn."

Boot camp attendees found they *liked* going to the gemba, and working on actual problems. Waste walks were a revelation. "This is fun but scary," John Winter admitted. "I didn't know we were so screwed up."

John also came up with the boot camp's best line, in response to the question *What is Lean?*

"Lean," he told us, "means don't be a dumbass." Interesting drawing, too.

Taylor Motors had a cavalier disregard for our most precious resource—time. So we always started and ended on time, even if people were absent. We used red and yellow cards to manage presentation length. You had five minutes to tell your story. At four minutes you got the yellow card, at five minutes you got the red card and had to stop. If you can't tell your story in five minutes, you don't understand it.

"What's the one thing you can't buy, rent, or lease—at any price?" I'd ask. Executives looked at me in silence. I quoted from Shakespeare's Richard II.

I wasted time. Now time doth waste me. See Figure 7.1.

Sarah's influence again. We'd seen the play off-Broadway and it got to me. Richard II is a regal figure but he's wasteful in his spending habits, unwise in his choice of advisors, and out of touch with his country and people. He spends too much of his time pursuing the latest fashions, spending money on his pals, and raising taxes to fund his pet wars. In his arrogance, he betrays an innocent family, that of Henry Bolingbroke, and pays the price.

FIGURE 7.1   I Wasted Time . . .

Our second wave of boot camps would begin next week. The morning of day one, attendees would report how they'd *applied* the previous session's learning. It was an important test, and I encouraged senior management to attend—to see where their people were. Many would be unprepared—at Taylor Motors you never have to *apply* what you learn. They'd have to report out, regardless; many would be embarrassed.

Our strategy deployment activities were also bearing fruit, some of it misshapen perhaps, but better than the crop of previous years. With help from Becky and Antonio, departments translated Chloe's design goals into focused activities and objectives that made sense for the *zone*. We stopped trying to do everything. Planning trees were no longer mangroves.

Command-and-control types pushed back. "Hey, where's *my* pet project?" We stood our ground. "We can't do everything. We have to trust people in each zone to pick what's important." The command-and-control types grumbled but generally backed off. They knew Rachel had my back.

After a rough start, visual management started to take root. Our obeya rooms made hot spots more visible, which triggered problem solving. We weren't good at getting to root cause yet, but at least we were focused. Zone teams also began setting up obeyas. A3s and one-page dashboards began to replace PowerPoint decks. Daily stand-up meetings became crisper. You had five minutes to tell your story. People learned to leave the boring parts out.

Yokoten was lagging though. Elaine Yamamoto had written a good A3 and deployed it well, but got plenty of resistance. I felt she was at root cause—dysfunctional mental models—and her countermeasures were reasonable. "Stay the course," I told her. "It takes time to change thinking."

At Taylor Motors, shared learning meant putting so-called best practices on the company intranet. Best practices were typically long and boring, and described *what* people did—not *why*. The valuable part, the *rationale*, was lost. It was akin to trying to eat the clam shell—after discarding the succulent core!

Yokoten also meant mentorship, which, sadly, was foreign to Taylor Motors. In the old days, mentorship and the gemba were revered. I thought of the practical dreamers who built the company, tinkering with stuff on the lab bench, and then trying it out the next day on the factory floor, students all around, soaking in the learning. But we'd lost it. In the long term, yokoten would make or break us.

Andy and I maintained a dialogue on leadership. "What's the role of the leader?" Andy had asked.

For once, I knew the answer, "To get business results."

"And what else?"

"To build capability—of people, processes, and equipment."

Andy raised his eyebrows—*please continue*.

"You always talk about *big heart*, which means the leader must reinforce values."

Andy nodded. "The leader's job is to get business results, build capability, and reinforce values. Two and three are the means to achieving one. Values provided constancy of purpose. Life is a marathon. This you know; you are a Greek!"

I laughed, and remembered our trip to Greece last summer. Sarah, the girls, and I joined my brother Harry and his family on Corfu. We also spent an afternoon at the plain of Marathon, where long ago the outnumbered Greeks defeated the Persians and preserved Western civilization. Sarah quoted Lord Byron, "The mountains look on Marathon, and Marathon looks on the sea. . . ."

"You are daydreaming," said Andy. "Next question, how do leaders build capability and reinforce values?"

"By acting like a sensei. By helping people learn for themselves."

"Do you mean through *empowerment*?"

"No," I replied. "I don't like this 'I'm okay, you're okay' stuff. Leaders define direction and suggest the means. Then they lead people through their actions."

Andy nodded again. "What you do, is what you get, Tom-san—the water ring model of leadership."

"I'm not sure I understand," He drew it out for me. See Figure 7.2.

"The formal power of leaders is quite low," Andy explained. "You can fire or demote team members. You can hold back a bonus and so on. But this is a negative power and not very effective. Much more effective is the ability to create *atmosphere*. Leaders do this with their behavior. What do leaders do every day? What is important to them? That is what team members will do."

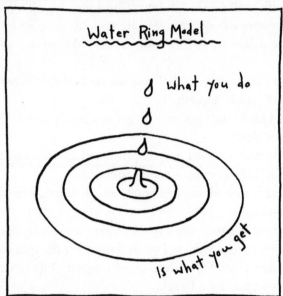

FIGURE 7.2   Water Ring Model of Leadership

I was silent. As in the old Greek proverb, a fish rots from the head. The condition of the gemba reflects the management team. I had a flash of insight. "Sensei, seems to me there are four types of leaders." I drew it out. See Figure 7.3.

"You've always taught me to manage as if I have no power, which has always puzzled me. Now it makes sense. I'm the chief engineer for the Chloe project. As a Shusa, I have responsibility, but little authority. Yet it seems to be working. We should apply this principle more broadly. Even if you *have* authority, lead as if you *don't*. That way you compel people to get involved, and to learn."

Then, another eureka. "Why, it's a *pull* system!"

Andy smiled. "Maybe too much bourbon last night, Tom-san."

All things considered, our supplier visits went well. They're understandably reluctant to cooperate. As one supplier exec told me last month, "You expect us to open our kimono—after the way you've treated us?"

Through these visits we hoped to regain supplier trust. I explained that Chloe represented a new approach for Taylor Motors. We were

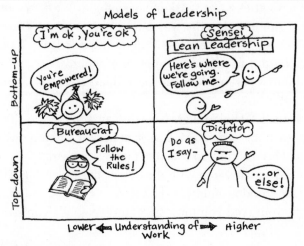

Copyright © 2010 by Lean Pathways Inc.

FIGURE 7.3   Models of Leadership

committed to helping suppliers improve, for our mutual benefit. Rachel Armstrong had sent a letter to all Chloe suppliers, confirming that for the first six months after an improvement, they would keep all savings generated thereby. Thereafter, we would share savings equally.

Both electronics suppliers we visited had big problems, many caused by us. We changed our schedules so often they were forced to carry extra finished goods inventory. We forced them to make costly, time-consuming design changes, simply to comply with our internal specs—reengineering for its own sake. Moreover, we often *penalized* them for improvement by grabbing any cost savings for ourselves. "Give it to me. That's *mine!*"

In any event, by late afternoon we were heading into Boston to meet Sam Sparrow. Andy, a Red Sox and Daisuke Matsuzaka fan, wanted to see Fenway Park. Sam's office was nearby and he had graciously offered to pick up Fenway tour tickets and meet us there. Had the Red Sox been in town, we'd have been out of luck.

We arrived early so I decided to give Andy a tour of Beantown. He found the nickname puzzling. I explained its origin, the molasses, bean and rum years, as we drove east along Beacon Street. To our right, elegant row homes, stylish shops, and cobblestone streets. To

our left, the Charles River sparkling in sunlight. We drove all the way
to Boston Common. On the way back, I pointed out *The Athenian
Bar & Grill*, my Uncle Pericles' old place. Uncle Perry had sold the
place to a cousin and retired to enjoy his grandkids.

I pulled into a parking lot near the ballpark. "This is a great town,
despite the Red Sox."

Andy grinned. "The Yankees have difficulty in Fenway, Tom-san."

"Don't rub it in." The 2004 American League Championship Series
collapse had been a blow to Yankees fans everywhere.

We walked up the ramp with the other pilgrims. A big fellow with
an open face stood grinning at the top of the ramp. "Saito-san, how
good to see you! And you must be Tom Papas. Welcome to Fenway
Park!"

We exchanged greetings and kibitzed a while, Sam and Andy catching up on Toyota scuttlebutt. It was clear they'd deeply discussed
Toyota's troubles and were aligned on root cause: Business growth
had outstripped the company's ability to grow senseis. Like Dean
Formica, Sam had volunteered to help build Toyota University and
reground the company in its fundamentals.

"Thanks for getting the tickets, Sam," I said.

"My pleasure," Sam replied. "I've heard a lot about you, Tom. It's
great to meet you. And it's great to see Saito-san. He changed the way
I look at the world."

"You and me both," I put in.

"Can Toyota recover its mojo?" I asked.

Sam nodded. "They're a brilliant company. My gut says they're
going to bear down and get stronger."

The Fenway tour was fun. History, great players, the Green
Monster—how can you go wrong? I took some more razzing about
the Yankees. We were all in a good mood as we walked across the
street to the Boston Beer Works for dinner.

Sam and Andy started with Boston Garden golden ale; I went with
the Beantown nut-brown lager. On Sam's recommendation, we all
ordered the clam chowder and pan-roasted salmon with malt top-
ping. "You won't be sorry," he said.

Sam raised his glass. "Welcome to Boston. Congratulations on
NJMM's success, Tom. Andy shared some of your adventures
with me."

We clinked beer mugs. I took a pull on my lager. "Chloe is a much bigger challenge."

"I'm anxious to see how it turns out. Big implications."

Andy nodded. "It is very important that Chloe succeed. Sam-san, you may be able to help."

"I'm interested in complex systems," Sam told us. "How they fail, and how they succeed."[1]

He had my interest. "Taylor Motors is a complex system, Sam. Why do you think the last incarnation failed?"

He pulled out a tattered notebook. "Let's go back in time to Taylor Motors in 1950. What do Sales, Marketing, Engineering, IT, Materials, Human Resources, and the other divisions look like?"

Andy closed his eyes and appeared to be meditating. I thought it over. "Well, for a start, each division is smaller and less complex. In fact, some divisions, like IT, don't even exist."

Sam nodded. "In 1950 Taylor Motors comprised comparatively few and shallow silos. How did these silos coordinate their activities?"

Sam had evidently learned Andy's questioning approach. "Informally," I replied. "Collegially."

"That's right. Now let's fast-forward. Describe Taylor Motors today."

"Many more silos," I answered, "each deeper and much more complex. IT, for example, is a universe. Our cars are wired like jets. Materials used to mean galvanized steel, simple rubber, and plastics. Now it means exotic alloys, advanced composite plastics, and nanotechnology."

Sam drew it out. See Figure 7.4.

"And how do these deep, complex, and numerous silos align their activities today?" Sam asked.

My head began doing the rumba. *Our alignment process hadn't changed.* We were still aligning informally—no wonder we were enveloped in fog.

---

[1] This chapter is informed and inspired by the work of my friend and colleague, Dr. Steven Spear. For a deeper discussion, I highly recommend Dr. Spear's work, including his recent book, *Chasing the Rabbit* (New York: McGraw-Hill, 2009).

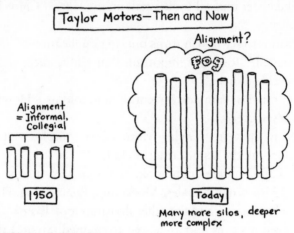

FIGURE 7.4 Taylor Motors—Then and Now

The waiter brought out steaming clam chowder and another round of beer.

"A powerful image," I said. "So why did Taylor Motors fail?"

"We've been taught the 'weak-link-in-the-chain' metaphor," Sam replied. "But it's not rich enough to describe complex systems. A spider web is a better metaphor."

He drew it out. "A complex system fails when the wrong combination of filaments fails, at the wrong time. This was true in the Challenger and Columbus space shuttle disasters, at Three Mile Island—and at Taylor Motors. To avoid catastrophic failure, we need to continually fix broken filaments, like a spider does." See Figure 7.5.

I was silent. Sam had provided a lens that brought the Lean system into sharp focus. Standards, visual management, and other Lean tools made problems, in other words, broken web filaments, *visible*—so that we could continually fix them. Involvement, mentorship, and atmosphere enabled problem solving.

I looked over at Andy. "You son-of-a-gun, how did Toyota figure this out?"

Andy opened his eyes. "Through trial and error. Ohno-san kept experimenting."

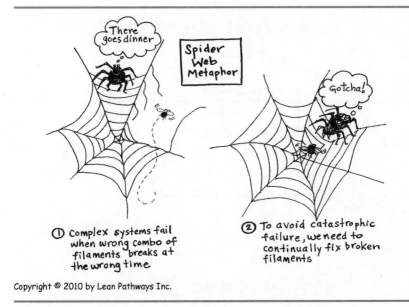

FIGURE 7.5   How Complex Systems Fail—and Succeed

"So leadership," Sam continued, "is a process of *discovery*—not compliance. The leader has to create an open, questioning, freewheeling atmosphere: *What did we discover is broken today—and how do we fix it?*"

"And how do we *share the learning*?" I added, remembering our yokoten struggles. Then, it hit me. "Isn't that the remedy to Big Company Disease? Isn't that how we dispel the fog?" I drew it out on my napkin. See Figure 7.6.

"Very good, Tom-san," Andy said. "But how do you discover what is broken? How can we *see* problems?"

"That's the key question," Sam agreed. "Nature gives us some clues. How do complex natural systems achieve order and stability? For example, how does a flock of migratory birds fly south every year to the correct destination, with minimum hassle?"

It was a poser. Were birdbrains superior to Taylor Motors' brains?

"Biologists have found that birds do it by applying *simple rules*," Sam went on. "Don't hit anything. Stay in the middle of the flock. Try to go in the same direction as the other birds."

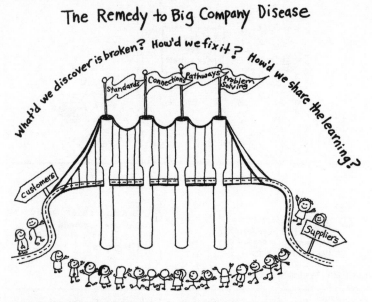

Copyright © 2010 by Lean Pathways Inc.

FIGURE 7.6 The Remedy to Big Company Disease

The implications hung in the air like ripe fruit. The waiter brought out our salmon, which gave off a malt and sesame aroma.

I took another pull on my beer. "So by applying simple rules we can create order in complex systems . . . A lot of people believe it takes bigger and faster computers."

Sam nodded, sampling a piece of salmon. "Computers often make things worse."

"The countermeasure to complexity," Andy commented," is *not* more complexity."

I tucked into dinner. I liked Sam Sparrow and sensed he would be a good friend. I silently thanked Andy, again.

"So what are the rules whereby complex organizations can achieve order and stability?" I asked.

"There are four," said Sam. "I learned them while working with Mr. Saito. They deal with standards, connections, pathways, and problem solving. I'll draw them out on these napkins."

The Four Rules

| Standards | Connections | Pathways | Problem Solving |

□ Content
□ Sequence
□ Time &
□ Expected outcome:
Safety, quality, delivery, cost
Embedded tests show Good/NG

Connections between customers & suppliers are:
□ Direct
□ Binary
□ Self-diagnostic

Pathways for products and services are
□ Simple
□ Prespecified
□ Self-diagnostic

Problem Solving should be done:
□ Under guidance of a teacher
□ At the lowest possible level
□ Using scientific Method

FIGURE 7.7 The Four Rules

Here are my subsequent renditions of Sam's drawings. (He kindly gave me all his drawings.) See Figure 7.7.

The Four Rules made intuitive sense and were informed by the mental models I'd internalized: standards, PDCA, problems are gold, pull, jidoka, leaders are senseis, respect for people, and so on. Each rule built on the last. Collectively, they entailed zooming out from point kaizen to system kaizen. We begin by standardizing different points in our system—*point kaizen*. Then we connect standardized processes—*flow kaizen*. Finally, we define the pathways along which products or services would flow—*system kaizen*.

"This is powerful, Sam," I said. "Rules one, two, and three tell you where the spider web is broken. Rule four tells you how to fix it."

"Exactly," Sam replied. "Because the web is big and filaments keep breaking, *everybody* has to know how to solve problems. There's no shame in having problems."

"The only shame is in *denying* you have them," I said.

I thought about all the executive meetings I'd sat through. That strange atmosphere of unreality; execs sitting in dense fog, pretending they knew what was going on.

We had key lime pie and coffee for desert. My head was now doing the meringue. We discussed examples of the Four Rules in a range of industries. Sam told us health care was now his primary focus. He gave us frightening examples of hospital dysfunction. I shared my fears that my dad might become another statistic. Sam said he didn't blame me and suggested things we might do to lessen the risk. In particular, we needed to confirm each drug, each procedure, dad received in advance. Apparently, my dry cleaner uses a more elaborate system to track shirts than most hospitals use to track treatment. Dad was going in next week for another series of checks. I made a note to call my brother Harry and make a plan.

The evening drew to a close. I had pages of notes and drawings, which I would summarize for the team. We could have talked into the early morning. Andy suggested we reflect on what we'd learned, and begin a dialogue. "You have much to teach each other—and to teach me!"

"He learns from our mistakes," Sam joked.

We gave Sam a lift to his house in Brookline and drove to the airport Marriott. We'd missed our flight and it was worth it. My head was buzzing. "Sensei, we need to include the Four Rules in our boot camps and kaizen activity."

"The timing is good, Tom-san. We're ready for management system kaizen."

"Where do we start?" I asked.

"With the customer—with marketing."

"That's what I was afraid of."

I called Sarah from the hotel and described the day's adventures. "Sam Sparrow is the real deal. I think he's going to be a great friend to us."

"Sounds like it," Sarah said. "Do you think his ideas apply to education?"

"You can ask him personally. We have an open invitation. In fact, he said he'll take us to a Red Sox game!"

"But we're Yankees fans. Tom, how *could* you . . ."

I laughed. "You'll never guess where we're taking Lean next . . . Marketing, Madison Avenue!"

"Leaning out the Mad Men . . . this I have to see!"

IMPLEMENTATION CHECKLIST

1. Help leaders at all levels develop a deep understanding of the Four Rules by applying the learn-by-doing principal.
2. Make checking and improving standards, connections, and pathways part of a leader's responsibility.
3. Base leader compensation packages on their ability to develop problem solvers.
4. Deploy the Four Rules in administrative areas such as Marketing, Design, IT, and HR, where they are harder to implement and sustain.

STUDY QUESTIONS

1. What is a standard? Draw out your answer[2] using as few written words as possible.
2. Give three examples of embedded tests in
   a. Your workplace (e.g., a temperature sensor in a hospital autoclave sterilizer).
   b. Outside work (e.g., a necessary field in an online form).
3. Give three examples of direct, binary connections between a customer and a supplier:
   a. At work (e.g., a digital replenishment signal between a consumer goods distribution center and the retailer's shelf).
   b. Outside work (e.g., ordering a laptop computer online directly from the manufacturer).
4. Give three examples of simple, prespecified pathways
   a. At work (e.g., standardized pick route in a warehouse).
   b. Outside work (e.g., bus service).
5. What does self-diagnostic mean? Draw it out.
6. What is the scientific method? Draw it out.

---

[2] *The Back of the Napkin,* by Dan Roam (New York: Penguin, 2008), illustrates the power of visual thinking and provides tips on how to get started.

Chapter 8 Marketing—Leaning Out the Mad Men

I was in the CMM paint shop doing my weekly waste walk when my BlackBerry began buzzing. A voice like a ripe orange rolled out of the speaker. "Tom Papas, how the hell are you? Art Juna here."

"Mr. Juna," I stammered, "I'm honored . . ."

"Call me Art," he said. "Listen, just heard your Chloe team is moving into marketing. Be tough on them! They're good people but have lacked oversight for a long time. We do a full-court press before spending a few hundred million on design, but spend *four billion* a year in marketing with hardly a check. I'm getting to know them. Been doing some TV spots. Marketing can benefit from your Lean approach. Jill Henderson is with me."

Jill Henderson was SVP of Marketing. I'd heard she was okay. "Thanks, Art. I agree there's a ton of opportunity in marketing. We can make an impact just by applying the basics."

"Damned straight," said Juna. "Ed Deming taught me the PDCA cycle 35 years ago! It's just good management, for heaven's sake! But the mantra in Taylor Motors seems to be PFPF."

"Not sure I follow . . . "

"Plan-Fail-Plan-Fail!" he laughed. "Let's turn that around. Anyhow, I'm looking forward to meeting you in person. I like what I hear about you. The Chloe launch is shaping up. Six months to go. I want you to kick ass and take names! You have any difficulty, you call me!"

And with that, he was gone. I was grinning the rest of the day.

When Benny Walton joined the team, I told him I was clueless about marketing. "All I know I learned on *Mad Men*."[1]

"It's a great series," he laughed, "but things have changed since 1960."

Bennie's become my marketing sensei. He gives homework; we discuss it, and, where possible, do a go see. Luckily, Benny has plenty of contacts in the marketing industry. I'm beginning to understand this mysterious world.

In fact, every Friday we have a "lunch and learn" on a topic of interest: Marketing, Design, Engineering, Supply Chain, our dealer network, led by a different team member. I teach the Four Rules. (The blind leading the blind, I joked.) The format's simple: prereading, 30-minute presentation, group activity, and homework. It's our team's yokoten.

I've learned that marketing is about *connecting* with the customer. Connections need to be *direct, binary,* and *self-diagnostic.*

Direct means personal and experiential—not abstract. Market surveys, focus groups, and the like are necessary—but not sufficient. You have to feel the customer's need in your gut. Andy told us about the Sienna Shusa who drove 50,000 miles through every U.S. state and Canadian province, in all sorts of terrain and weather, to gain this gut feel.

Binary means Yes/No, Red/Green, and entails boiling things down to their essence, translating all our market intelligence, experience, and intuition into the fundamental few specifications, as Mr. Suzuki, the renowned Lexus Shusa, did when launching Toyota's premier brand a decade ago. Lexus' hoshin was *the pursuit of perfection.* Mr. Suzuki and the Lexus module teams boiled it down to a handful

---

[1] The acclaimed TV series set in a Madison Avenue advertising agency in the early 1960s.

of binary specs per zone. Collectively, they added up to a breakthrough experience in comfort and performance.

Self-diagnostic means building tests into our program so that problems become visible quickly. Bennie says market researchers are trained to do this very thing, but are often swamped by the daily chaos.

What is the work of marketing?[2] I like Bennie's mantra: *Listen, make good stuff, and tell them about it*. In other words, marketing work entails:

- Understanding what customers value.
- Communicating downstream to New Product Development.
- Communicate product benefits upstream to the public.

"Our marketers spend most of their time in the spin cycle," Bennie told me.

"What kind of waste will we find?"

"Delay, defect, and overprocessing waste are the big ones. We'll find unclear processes full of unnecessary steps and multiple redo loops. We'll see decision complexity and plenty of superstition—people guessing at answers and hoping for the best."

"I imagine there's a ton of knowledge waste." Bennie nodded. "We won't see team huddles, team boards, or focused kaizen. Ahead/behind status and hot spots will be invisible. In other words, a typical business process . . ."

"What mental models are common in marketing?" I asked.

"*Leader equals dictator* is the most common. Because things are chaotic, dictators get ahead. *Problems are garbage—bury them* is another common mental model. I remember one time a promotional campaign that went wrong. The boss, Reggie, had told people he *didn't want to hear bad news*. So people were freaking out. *Reggie won't like this. Reggie won't like this.* People were afraid to make the problem visible. So of course, it got buried and was never fixed properly." See Figure 8.1.

---

[2] I'm obliged to David Hughes for these and other insights into marketing. Many are based on his presentation, "Marketing and Lean," Lean Pathways Spring Conference, Toronto, May 2009.

FIGURE 8.1 Reggie Won't Like This

I shook my head. "Bet you wanted to smack Reggie in the head."

"He quit, thank God."

"Any other mental models, Bennie?"

"*Standards constrain creativity.* You know what I mean: *We are creative, beautiful people. Standards will only hold us back . . .* "

I nodded. Benny had pulled himself out of a chaotic childhood through guts, brains, and adherence to standards.

MARKETING BASICS

Marketing is the "management process responsible for identifying, anticipating, and satisfying customer requirements profitably" (Chartered Institute of Marketing). Marketing is a rich field that encompasses social science, psychology, math, economics, and anthropology. Although promotion is as old as civilization, marketing was invented during the Industrial Revolution, when mass producers needed better ways of connecting with the public.

Marketing functions typically comprise:

Research

- What does the customer value?
- What markets are we in? How big are they? How fast are they growing? Threats? Opportunities?
- What's our positioning?
- What are our competitors doing?
- How do their products compare with ours?

Product

- What products will we offer?
- Target customers?
- How will we reach our customers (distribution channels)?
- How should we price our products?
- How do we introduce and promote our products?
- What's our product mix? Do we have a good balance between cash cows, questions marks, stars, and dogs (BCG formulation)?

Market Communications

- How will we get our message to potential customers?
- What mix of advertising, promotions, Internet, viral marketing, and so forth, will we use?

Planning

- How will we create and keep customers?
- What's happening in our business environment?
- What are our strengths and weaknesses?
- What threats and opportunities do we see?
- How do we adjust our product, price, promotions, and distribution?

Brand Management

- Strong brands have the power of instant sales. (What's the value of a pair of Nike trainers without the logo?) Strong brands convey a message of confidence, quality, and reliability. A brand is a powerful tool for differentiating ourselves from the competition.
- How will we manage our brands?
- How are they currently perceived?
- Strengths? Weaknesses? Threats? Opportunities?

Other functions include Trade Marketing (to wholesalers and other intermediaries) and Direct Marketing (to the user).

Implications for Lean thinkers: Everything is a process, with customers, suppliers, inputs, and outputs. Focus on the underlying process and on customer-defined value. Everything else follows naturally.

Source: "Marketing and Lean," by David Hughes, Lean Pathways Spring Conference, Toronto, May 2009.

"*Don't stop production* is also common," Bennie continued. "*Hey, we've got some promotion space available, let's do what we did last month!* Big batch thinking is also common. Like the rest of our company, marketing loves monster data dumps—and seems averse to providing information in frequent, digestible batches."

Bennie paused. "I don't mean to sound so negative. We have good people—doing what they've been taught to do. They're just caught in this death spiral."

"Understood," I replied. "What about visual management, go see, and the scientific method?"

"Very little visual management—everything is 'in the computer.' Hierarchy is important, so *go see* is for grunts. PDCA is weak, especially the Check/Adjust phase. Marketing planning tends to be overly complex—lots of PowerPoint junk. Superstition is common, as I suggested, as is dependence on consultants. *We're losing market share—and it's not my fault. Get the consultants in!*"

"So no daily accountability process."

Benny shook his head. "We're lucky if there's a monthly check. It's usually a song and dance routine. You ask the kind of questions you ask at NJMM, people's heads would explode . . ."

"Smart, hard-working people," I summed up, "in chaotic, wasteful, invisible processes."

"And no expectation of regular improvement," Bennie added.

I was silent. "When marketing finally understands their mess, they'll get depressed. I remember how we felt at NJMM. We'll have to remember Mr. Saito's mantra. *Hard on the problem, easy on the people.*"

Bennie nodded. "The first few months may be tough."

"Where do we focus our marketing activity?" I asked "Where is Chloe most at risk?"

"Market research and marketing communication, these are the critical processes." Bennie answered. "Marketing is like chess. To make the right moves we need good intelligence and good communication. Do we understand the customer—and the competition? Not just the competition's product, but also how they're positioning it. We need quick, useful feedback we can act on. Is our message consistent across all our channels? Does it resonate with people? We're off to a promising start. Chloe is a cute name and our design tweaks seem bang on.

Can we also make the car *look* cute? I'm encouraged by the drawings coming out of design. Those new headlights look awesome!"

Benny could see three moves ahead. No wonder he was good at chess.

"Let's focus on marketing research and communication," I agreed. "What can I do?"

"Accelerate the boot camps. Marketing execs and Lean coordinators have to understand the basics," Bennie said. "And get marketing exec support."

"Will do. Thanks, Bennie. Full speed ahead."

Andy taught us that in marketing, as in design, engineering, and all business process areas, there is the *small* process and the *big* process— and there is waste associated with each.

The small process comprises the core processes of marketing. Waste here comprises the 7 + 1 wastes Bennie described. The big process entails the overall marketing system. Big process waste means "missing the sweet spot"; that is, not understanding what customers value, or not delivering corresponding products. The big process is informed by our mental models. See Figure 8.2.

"There are three types of customer *value*," Andy told us. "*Expected*, *Specified*, and *Delightful* value. We expect an automobile to start. We expect it to be comfortable and stay dry in a rainstorm. This is Expected value.

Two Types of Marketing Waste

Value

Knowledge · Motion · Waiting · Conveyance · Correction · over-processing · over-production · Inventory

Muda > 95%
Process Waste

Missing the Customer's Sweet Spot

FIGURE 8.2   Two Types of Marketing Waste

"Specified value is usually linear. The more we get, the happier we are. For example, cheaper and faster is better. Most companies understand these. But the most difficult to grasp is *Delightful* value, because sometimes not even the customer knows he or she values it!" See Figure 8.3.

Bennie and I mulled it over.

"Why is the iPod worth twice as much as other MP3 players?" Andy asked.

"Because of how the iPod makes you *feel*," said Bennie.

"Yes, Bennie-san. Apple grasps the situation better than its competitors. Apple designers develop their thinking by *living* as the customer lives. Shusas take the same approach."

"Sensei, it's too late to gain *that* level of understanding of Chloe customers," I said. "We have our list of Chloe improvements for this launch. But how do we build this kind of understanding into future models?"

"That is the Shusa's role," said Andy. "Your job, Tom-san, is to develop Shusa standardized work."

Like all our team members, I was keeping a journal for that very purpose. "Another question, sensei. Business process kaizen is about to accelerate, starting with marketing, and moving downstream into

FIGURE 8.3   Three Types of Customer Value

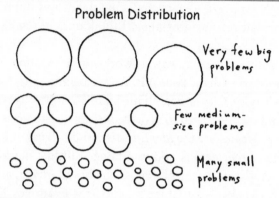

Problem Distribution

FIGURE 8.4   Problem Distribution

design, engineering, supply chain, and beyond. How do we ensure our kaizens are focused?"

Andy went to the whiteboard. "This is how problems are distributed in most organizations." See Figure 8.4.

"To ensure alignment," he continued, "we must act locally, but think globally." See Figure 8.5.[3]

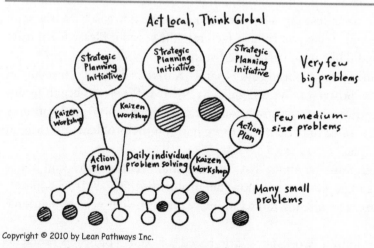

Act Local, Think Global

FIGURE 8.5   Act Local, Think Global

---

[3] *The Toyota Way Fieldbook*, by Jeffrey Liker and David Meier (New York: McGraw-Hill, 2005).

"Marketing's strategic focus is reducing delay and improving the quality of information," said Bennie. "I think our chosen kaizens are okay."

We began with a three-day kaizen workshop in Market Research, sponsored by Maria Chan, zone VP. Andy, Bennie, and I met with Maria in her Taylor City office. "Our team's purpose is reconnaissance," she told us. "We need to provide *intelligence* to decision makers. Our core processes are the *identification* and *solving* of marketing problems. The former entails understanding stuff like market potential and characteristics, business trends, our brand image, and the effect of design tweaks—like Chloe's lights, for example. The latter entails answering tough questions about the Four Ps. Like which levers should we pull to protect our share and increase margin?"

"It's a big game of Chess—or Go," Benny said, looking at Andy. They were teaching one another their favorite games.

"Exactly," Maria went on. "And without good research you can't see the board. I'd like to begin with our process for problem identification. It takes way too long."

Maria called in Alfredo Medina, her Lean coordinator. We exchanged greetings. Alfredo told us he had enjoyed his first boot camp and talked about visual management improvements his team had made.

"Bennie is leading a marketing kaizen next week," Maria said. "Alfredo, I'd like you to help facilitate the session. Please learn from Bennie. I'd like us to become self-sufficient."

"Maria, here's a heads up," I said. "Kaizen is difficult, especially in business processes. We struggled at NJMM. When we began to understand our current condition, we got depressed. Your team may have the same experience. Let's be hard on the problem and easy on the people."

"Been thinking about that," said Maria. "As Mr. Saito said in our boot camp, people are not the problem—they are the countermeasure. I've already talked to my team. But we'll need to reinforce it."

Our kaizen workshops are based on our Four-Step-Problem-Solving process:

1. Do I have a problem?
2. Do I know the cause?

3. Have I proven cause and effect?
4. Have I confirmed the countermeasures?

How does one learn virtue? Through repetition, Aristotle taught. To be a good musician, you practice the scales. To learn Lean, you also practice the basics. If you're open and stay with it, in time you'll internalize them. Then you can improvise as a jazz musician riffs on the underlying chords.

THE FOUR Ps OF MARKETING

Product, Price, Place, and Promotion define the "marketing mix" that we believe will optimize sales and profitability.

Product
- Design—In touch with target market?
- Features—In touch with target market?
- Quality—Consistent with other elements of marketing mix?
- Branding—How do we manage our brands to differentiate ourselves?

Price
- The only "P" that generates revenue.
- Fixed and variable costs?
- How price sensitive is the market (elasticity)?
- What's the competition doing?
- What's our costing objective? Profile and volume? Overall margin? To break into new markets? Other?
- Positioning—Where are we starting? Low to enter market, then higher? Other?
- Pricing strategy? Penetration? Skimming? Premium?

Place
- Where will we sell our product? Direct to public? Dealers? Other?
- Intensive (saturation), Exclusive, Selective?

Promotion
- Product life cycle: Introduction, Growth, Maturity, Decline.
- Expected length?

(continued)

> *(continued)*
> - Type of promotion per life cycle stage?
> - Advertizing, Internet, Sales Promotions, Other (viral, guerilla, etc.).
> - Message and media strategy?
>
> Collectively, the Four Ps define the "levers" we can pull to influence sales.
>
> Lean link: Everything is a process. The processes underlying the Four Ps determine the effectiveness of each lever.

Kaizen teams typically comprise six to eight people and are led by a sensei (Bennie) and an internal facilitator (Alfredo), whose job it is to learn the process. Bennie's marketing knowledge gave him credibility with attendees. I attended to deepen my understanding of marketing—and business process improvement.

Alfredo and the kaizen team used the Kaizen Workshop Profile Sheet[4] to scope out the problem, and the Target Sheet[5] to identify possible objectives.

The first question in the Four-Step-Problem-Solving-Process—*Do I have a problem?*—entails answering the following:

- What should be happening (WSBH)?
- What is actually happening (WAH)?

The team made the common mistake of defining the problem too broadly—delay in *all* market research. Bennie helped them focus on *delay in promotion research*, explaining that countermeasures generated thereby were likely to apply more widely. "Think global, act local," he reminded them.

WAH was an average delay of 26 days, with a range of 11 to 49 days. The team struggled with WSBH until Bennie explained the principle of Takt time. Demand for promotion research for the Chloe was estimated at 18 analyses per year. Takt time was defined as operating time divided by annual demand (240 days/18 = 13.3 days),

---

[4] This template can be downloaded at www.leanpathwaysinc.com.
[5] This template can be downloaded at www.leanpathwaysinc.com.

which was rounded to 13 days. Promotions research had to leave the "line" every 13 days. The team's problem statement was: *Delay in promotion research is hindering decision making.*

- *WSBH = 13 days*
- *WAH = 26 days*

TAKT TIME

Takt time = Operating time ÷ Demand

Takt time represents the frequency at which our product or service needs to leave the end of our "line," whether we're in manufacturing, health care, or marketing. Takt does not equal customer demand, a common misconception. In fact, Takt time is under our control. We can increase/decrease Takt time by increasing/decreasing operating time.

Takt time is our heartbeat, telling us at a glance where our bottlenecks are and whether we're ahead or behind. Takt helps us feel customer demand and is an important point of connection for an organization. Like True North, Takt gives us a shared purpose.

Takt time differs from cycle time, which is the actual time it takes to carry out a process. By comparing Takt and cycle times for a given operation we can identify bottlenecks and focus our improvement activity.

The second question—*Do I know the cause?*—entailed defining the three types of cause:

1. *Point of cause*—the physical time and location the abnormality is first observed.
2. *Direct cause*—"one why upstream" of the point of cause.
3. *Root cause*—several "whys" upstream of the point of cause and usually:
   - Inadequate standard
   - Inadequate adherence to standard
   - Inadequate system

Point of cause in our kaizen workshop was clearly the moment the decision maker found she lacked the necessary marketing information. Direct and root cause were not so clear. We learned that the promotions research process has six main steps, each with unclear standards and varying cycle times. Everyone had a different opinion as to what was causing delay.

Bennie introduced the Yamazume chart and asked the team to analyze their processes and develop corresponding charts. The fog began to clear. Process 6 was clearly the bottleneck—waiting and rework ate up six and five days, respectively. See Figures 8.6 and 8.7.

Bennie then introduced a process-mapping tool called SIPOC, which stands for Supplier-Inputs-Process-Outputs-Customer. "We have to get the process out of our heads and onto the wall—so we can think," he explained.

"Why don't we do a value stream map?" Alfredo asked.

"Value stream maps provide a snapshot of material and information flow," Bennie replied. "But they're not as effective for business processes, which are almost entirely about the latter." See Figure 8.8.

Question three—*Have I confirmed cause and effect?*—entails running experiments to test hypotheses. Question four—*Have I confirmed*

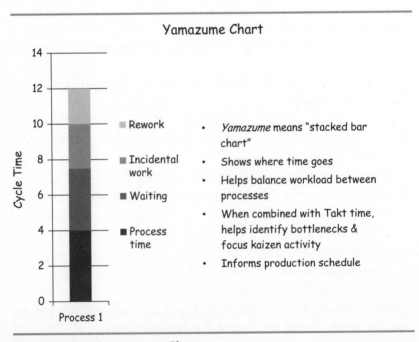

FIGURE 8.6 Yamazume Chart

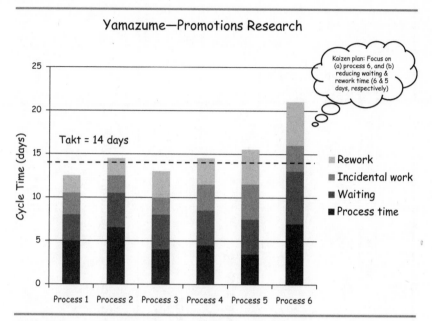

FIGURE 8.7   Yamazume—Promotions Research

the countermeasure?—begins with a so-called kaizen newspaper[6] explaining how we'll lock in countermeasures.

But the kaizen team didn't get past question two. They knew process six was the bottleneck but couldn't get to the root cause. So Bennie and Alfredo gave them homework and scheduled a follow-up session. In spite of the difficulties they'd faced, the team was eager for more. "This is hard," Alfredo said, echoing the group's sentiments, "but we learned a ton."

Bennie led a useful debrief with the team around the question, *Why is business process improvement so hard to do?*[7] The team's insights were a recurrent theme in the months to come. (See Figure 8.9.)

At their next kaizen session, the market research team got to at least one root cause, tested hypotheses, and locked in countermeasures that reduced cycle times from 26 to 20 days—a good improvement but still off target. In the months to come, the team

---

[6] This template can be downloaded at www.leanpathwaysinc.com.

[7] I'm obliged to Stuart Foster for these and other insights into business process kaizen. Many of them are based on his presentation, "Business Process Kaizen," Lean Pathways Spring Conference, Toronto, May 2009.

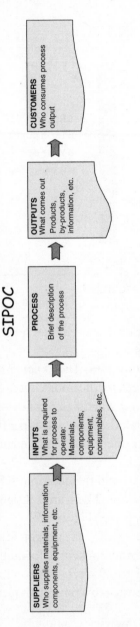

SIPOC

SUPPLIERS
Who supplies materials, information, components, equipment, etc.

INPUTS
What is required for process to operate: Materials, components, equipment, consumables, etc.

PROCESS
Brief description of the process

OUTPUTS
What comes out Products, by-products, information, etc.

CUSTOMERS
Who consumes process output

- Helps us understand business processes
- Useful for kaizen workshop or business problem scoping
- Start with customers
- Identify high-level wastes, issues, and problems
- Agree on processes that may need deeper dive

FIGURE 8.8 SIPOC

Source: "Business Process Kaizen," by Stuart Foster, Lean Pathways Spring Conference, Toronto, May 2009.

Why is business process improvement hard?

- Perception: ''Lean is only for Manufacturing''
- Who is my customer?
- What is value?
- Multiple customers
- Belief: ''We don't have processes''
- No process owners
- Less understanding of process & fewer measures
- Value & flow are invisible
- Work tailored to individuals —''This is my job . . .''
- Process cycle times are longer —harder to test for cause & effect
- Constant state of crisis leaves no time for improvement

FIGURE 8.9   Why Is Business Process Improvement Hard?
Source: "Business Process Kaizen," by Stuart Foster, Lean Pathways Spring Conference, Toronto, May 2009.

continued to work on market research lead time and eventually achieved, and held, their target. They came to understand Taiichi Ohno's famous aphorism: *Improvement is endless and eternal*—and its corollaries: Respect your people. Every day a little up. We don't have to be perfect.

We stayed the course in marketing—with executive development, a Lean Coordinator Network, and focused improvement activity. Lean thinking began to get traction. The fog began to clear and people relaxed.

We continued to get interference from Morgan and May. Petty stuff mostly, around budget and headcount rules. And Maude Beecher in Human Resources wouldn't promote the Lean coordinator position, or link it to a defined career path. Thankfully, almost all division heads funded the positions internally and encouraged strong people to apply.

Not long after our initial marketing kaizen, Andy and I were sipping bourbon at the Iron Horse. It was September and the kids were back in school. The Humpty Dumpty had had a prosperous summer. My dad's heart problems seemed to be in check. Andy's daughters, Yumi and Yamiko, had returned to Japan after a two-week stay.

Andy seemed content. Yumi had told me about Mrs. Yamamoto, a charming widow Andy had met at the Japanese Cultural Centre in Newark. I was pleased. It was tough to be alone.

I had some fun with Andy. "Let's see, Yumi, Yamiko, Yamamoto . . . are you doing a five why analysis, sensei?"

"You have much humor, Tom-san."

I changed the subject. "How'd we do in marketing?"

"Not bad," he replied. "Things are getting interesting."

We were going into design and engineering next. "Any words of wisdom, sensei?"

Andy took a sip of bourbon. "How to make *knowledge* flow?"

A week later I was sitting in an uptown Manhattan restaurant waiting for my ex-wife. Teal and I hadn't had lunch together since our divorce. It was a nice place—high ceilings, flowers, lots of light.

I looked out the window at the late summer cityscape. Another fine day. There she was, across the street. She had lost weight; she looked good. Teal walked into the restaurant, saw me. I stood up, smiled.

We shook hands awkwardly. "Thanks for the invite, Tom."

"You look great," I said.

"I'm working out five days a week. And . . . I've quit smoking!"

"I'm impressed. Thanks so much for coming. I'm nervous."

"I'm nervous, too," she admitted. "I haven't been very nice to you."

"Nor I to you. Maybe we can move past that now . . ."

She reached across the table and squeezed my hand. The butterflies eased; we relaxed and ordered lunch.

"How's it going with Sarah?" It was a hard question for her to ask.

"Sarah's great," I said. "Living with me is dysfunctioning her nerves."

Teal smiled. "I think she's good for you. You're much more relaxed. And she's kind to Helen and Sophie."

"How about you, seeing anybody?"

"Since our divorce I've been a recluse. But I'm starting to date again. Nothing serious. It's hard on the girls though. By now they're used to sharing Daddy with Sarah. But they've always had Mommy to themselves."

"Anything I can do?"

"I may ask you to take the girls from time to time. I've been focused entirely on them. I need a life of my own."

"You're a wonderful mom. I'd love more time with the girls."

We went on like that, talking about work, parents, New York. I remembered that once upon a time we had liked each other. All our anger seemed pointless.

I reached across the table and took her hand. "I don't want us to fight anymore. You've done a wonderful job with Sophie and Helen. I respect you and I want us to be friends. Anything you need, any time, please call me."

Her eyes were moist. "That would be nice, Tom."

IMPLEMENTATION CHECKLIST

1. Develop and teach a standardized approach to business process improvement. Integrate it with your problem-solving approach.
2. Recognize the obstacles to business process improvement and make a countermeasure plan.
3. Build the capability of your internal Lean coordinators by having them cofacilitate kaizen workshops with your senseis.
4. Take the long view with respect to business process improvement. Recognize that it will take longer for Lean to develop roots here than in the factory.
5. Teach your executives and Lean coordinators the basics of business process improvement. Pull in tools like Yamazume and SIPOC, as required. Emphasize the thinking that supports the tools.

STUDY QUESTIONS

1. Give at least one example from your industry of
   a. Expected value
   b. Specified value
   c. Delightful value
2. Describe your company's approach to business process improvement.
   a. What are its strong points? What are its weak points?
   b. How might you improve it?

3. Do a Yamazume chart for at least one process in your zone of control.

   a. Any insights, reflections?

   b. How might you improve this process?

4. Do a SIPOC chart for at least one business process in your organization.

   a. Any insights, reflections?

   b. How might you improve this process?

5. Identify at least one obstacle to business process improvement in your organization.

   a. Identify possible countermeasures

Chapter 9 Design and Engineering— Making Knowledge Flow

"Sam-san, Kurt-san, what do you see?"

Sam Hendry, Kurt Schaeffer, Andy, and I were doing a visual management walk in the engine test lab at the Design Centre. The lab measured about 10,000 square feet, had high ceilings and glass walls. The walls and floors were bare concrete.

There were 15 engine test cells—glass-and-metal structures sprouting pneumatic, hydraulic, and electronic cables. Only three were in operation even though the lab was crammed with engines. Technicians sat at desks around the perimeter. Not much was happening.

Sam and Kurt were our team leaders in Design and Engineering, respectively. They were preparing for upcoming boot camps with executives and Lean coordinators, and had asked for help with problem selection. As I mentioned, boot camps entailed practical problem solving in the gemba. Engine testing, central to new technology like Chloe's HEV engine, was a good place to start.

It was late fall and the financial tsunami continued to recede. The economy was showing tentative signs of life. People were "prairie-dogging"—poking their heads out, to see if it was safe. But they weren't buying cars—not like they used to. North America wouldn't see annual car sales of 16 million again for a long time. Our most optimistic internal forecast called for 12 million. Like everybody else, we'd have to adapt to lower volumes and slow growth.

"I see equipment, test chambers, engines," Sam replied.

"What is the engine lab's work this week? Are they ahead or behind?"

"We have no idea," said Kurt.

"Is this amount of inventory normal or abnormal? What is the bottleneck process? Is it fully loaded?" Andy continued. "Who are the engine lab's customers? What are their expectations?"

Kurt shrugged. There was no way to answer any of these questions.

"When we ask test lab team members these questions, what do they say?" Andy went on.

"They say it's all in the *computer*," Sam answered. "And when we check, we often find the computer is wrong."

It was a recurrent theme with business processes. Information was always in a box called the computer.

Andy walked over to a test cell surrounded by HEV engines. "Let's talk about the Four Rules. How would you rate Standards, Connections, Pathways, and Improvement in this lab?"

"I'll start with Rule 1—Standards," Sam Hendry said. "Content, sequence, and expected outcome are unclear for the test cell start-up and changeover processes. There appear to be embedded tests but they're sometimes ignored. Remember that technician who discounted the temperature gauge? 'That's always in the red,' he told us."

"Connection to customer—Rule 2—doesn't appear to be direct or binary," Kurt Schaeffer said. "Customer requirements are unclear. Looks like they do simple pass/fail tests. Priorities are unclear—all projects are treated the same. Nobody seems to know what's in the pipeline."

Sam nodded. "There are three main project types—major launches, model refreshes, and experimental work. As Kurt says, they're all treated the same, and the test is pass/fail. There's no look-ahead process, so we never know what's coming. It's hard to develop any rhythm."

"Pathways—Rule 3—seem convoluted," Sam went on. "Engines bounce around from test cell to test cell. There's no prescribed flow path. If we understood customer demand better, we could assign high runners to specific pathways and test cells, and set min/max inventory levels. We'd have a better chance at flow. I'll bet we could cut test lead times in half."

"So standards, connections, and pathways are unclear," Andy summed up. "What kind of waste does this create?"

"Delay and overprocessing," I answered, "as in Marketing."

Kurt pointed to the engines all around us. "Work in process and conveyance waste, too. Heavy engines get shuffled round randomly."

Andy nodded. "How would you assess Rule 4—improvement?"

"There's little evidence of root cause problem solving," Kurt replied. "No team boards or report-out areas. The walls and floors are completely bare. It's not surprising. If standards, connections, and pathways are weak, we won't *see* the problems. You can't fix what you can't see."

We stood there soaking it in. Kurt was scribbling in his notebook.

Andy changed the subject. "What's the *purpose* of Design and Engineering?"

"To create useful knowledge,"[1] Kurt answered.

"And to create profitable value streams," Sam added. "It's not enough to create a great product; you also have to design the value stream that will build it."

Solid answers. Kurt and Sam had done their homework.

"How do we define value in Design and Engineering?" Andy went on.

"Value is team members creating useful knowledge," Kurt replied. "Everything else is waste. In design, knowledge waste is the most damaging."

Andy agreed. "Shared learning—*yokoten*—is critical. If there is no learning we are in big trouble. I would like you both to talk to Sam Sparrow about yokoten . . ."

---

[1] *Lean Product and Process Development*, by Allen C. Ward. (Cambridge, MA: Lean Enterprise Institute, 2007).

Copyright © 2010 by Lean Pathways Inc.

FIGURE 9.1   What Causes Knowledge Waste in Design?

"Can you tell us more about knowledge waste?" Sam asked.

For once Andy answered a question directly. "There are two important causes. Disrupting *flow* and *absorption* of knowledge. What can disrupt flow of knowledge?" See Figure 9.1.

"*Physical* barriers are the most obvious," Kurt answered, "which is why our obeya has no barriers. Engineering and design software systems often don't talk to one another—that's a barrier, too. There's also a barrier between professionals and tradespeople. The prototype shops say they rarely see engineers."

"Good examples, Kurt-san. Constant reorganization is another barrier. Design and engineering depend on personal relationships, on trust built over many shared projects. If we continually change organizational structure and break up project teams, these connections are broken. Very bad! Same thing with constant requests for information. Designers spend too much time making or preparing for presentations. For what purpose? Because a senior manager is curious . . ."

"It's another expression of command and control," Sam said. "*I'm going to ask for unnecessary reports—just because I can.*"

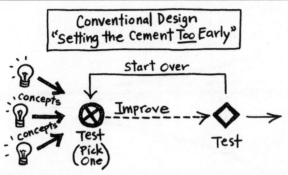

FIGURE 9.2   Conventional Design—"Setting the Cement Too Early"

"Here are some other barriers to knowledge flow," I offered. "Endless e-mail, overly complex written procedures nobody can follow. Have you seen our design system manuals?"

"How about overburden?" Kurt put in. "Each designer has 20 or more projects on the go. Do we understand Design Takt time, capacity, or bottlenecks?"

Andy nodded. "Now please provide examples of disruptions to knowledge *absorption*."

"PowerPoint junk is the most obvious," said Sam. "Constant reorganization and endless review meetings are another. Lab test reports are one, too. Almost all of them are pass/fail—which teach us little. Mr. Saito showed me corresponding Toyota reports, which include learning points, relevant drawings, and trade-off curves—all on one page. Unlike our labs, Toyota labs typically test to *failure*—to learn as much as possible."

Andy went to the whiteboard again. "Here is conventional design." See Figure 9.2.

"And here is Lean design," Andy said. "Who can explain the difference?" See Figure 9.3.

"The first drawing reflects our current design process," Sam said. "We force the most critical decision—the basic design concept—before we have any meaningful data. When our initial choice comes up short, there's a last-minute scramble for alternatives. Result: high

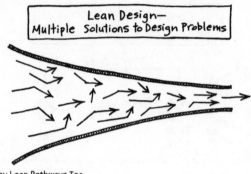

Copyright © 2010 by Lean Pathways Inc.

FIGURE 9.3   Lean Design—Multiple Solutions to Design Problems

cost, compromised quality, and delays. The second way is called *set-based concurrent design.*"[2]

"We choose suppliers the same way," I said. "Through an early bid process—before we have specs, and before we know what the supplier can do."

"It's natural to want to reduce uncertainty," Andy said. "But the Design leader's job is to keep people from making decisions too *early*. People believe that looking at one alternative is cheaper than looking at multiple solutions. *Not true!* Learn with quick and cheap experiments. Let each group develop multiple solutions and let them converge on a design that hits the customer's sweet spot." See Figure 9.4.

We absorbed it in silence. Andy was describing a design process based on different mental models and skills. We'd have to inhale and exhale yokoten. We'd have to be comfortable doing quick and dirty experiments and sharing learning with simple media like A3 reports. Our prototype shops and other supporting groups would have to shorten cycle times and strengthen customer connections. Our reports and review meetings had to be short, succinct, and focused on exceptions. We'd have to swarm problems made visible.

I looked around the test lab, took in the bare walls, sleepy atmosphere, and idle machinery. "This is going to take a long time," I said.

---

[2] Ibid.

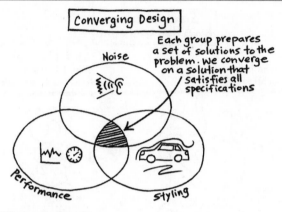

Copyright © 2010 by Lean Pathways Inc.

FIGURE 9.4   Converging Design

Andy nodded, and then changed the subject. "We need to apply Takt, flow, and pull in Design. What is the effect of information batch size on Design?"

"Design's product is useful information," Kurt replied. "Big batches of information are hard to digest. They slow down both flow and absorption of knowledge. If you release all your drawings in big batches, for example, users are overwhelmed. '*I don't need all the drawings—just that one! And I needed it last week!*' Same thing if your review meetings are daylong marathons each quarter."

"Same thing applies to experimentation," Sam added. "Quick, small batch experiments provide useful knowledge fast. But we like big, complex experiments that take a long time. It reflects our big-batch approach to innovation. We're always looking for the home run."

"The irony," said Kurt "is that major breakthroughs are usually the result of many small breakthroughs over a long period of time."

"Luck is where opportunity meets preparation,"[3] Sam added.

Andy nodded. "So how do we reduce batch size in Design?"

"We have to make knowledge digestible," I replied. "Drip, drip, drip . . . as opposed to the fire hose. Small, quick experiments toward multiple solutions to design problems—and peak learning. Singles and doubles that keep the runner moving. Occasionally, we'll hit one

---

[3] Attributed to Seneca, the Roman philosopher.

FIGURE 9.5   Small Batch versus Big Batch Learning

out of the park. Fine, but let's make sure we have runners on base. Similarly, design reviews should be short, stand-up meetings where we share what we've learned. Drip, drip, drip. . . ." (See Figure 9.5.)

"I like those images," Kurt said. "We're like the selfish slugger who swings for the fences, when a single will do; who cares more about personal success than team success. And our phase gate reviews are like the endless lineups you get at airports . . ."

I nodded. "To run quick experiments in our test labs we need quick changeover, good machine uptime, and visual management—the things we've learned in manufacturing. Let's *share* that learning. Let's connect Antonio with the right Design people."

"You got it, boss," said Sam. "This is really helpful. We have what we need for our boot camp. We'll focus on basic problems—delay, rework, and overprocessing. When they're ready, we'll dig into deeper stuff."

"By the way," I said, "how is strategy deployment working in Design and Engineering?"

"Better than expected," Kurt replied. "Too many objectives and activities still, but we're much more focused than we were. Chloe's overall design objectives are much more visible. People seem to have absorbed the *think global—act local* concept. A3s and dashboards are catching on. Review meetings and reports are getting shorter. People like the obeya concept, and especially the short, stand-up meetings. Designers and engineers appreciate the freedom Chloe's given them."

"How is the Lean Coordinator Network going?"

"It's still early," Sam said. "Most groups have good people in the role. They're teaching our basic curriculum and starting to learn from one another."

I was pleased. We were following the recipe and laying the foundation. I looked over at Andy. "Sensei, I believe you have more to say about Design and Engineering . . ."

"We have talked about flow," Andy said. "Now we need to understand Takt, pull, and kaizen in Design." Andy began by differentiating between "small process and big process" kaizen. Small process kaizen, Andy explained, addresses tactical questions like: *How do we improve machine uptime and changeover time in the engine test lab?* Our boot camps and kaizen workshops *start* here.

Big process kaizen is the executive's purview, and is focused on the management system. Our boot camps *go* there but it would take a couple of years. Big process kaizen requires a deep understanding of Takt time and of the laws of production physics.

Takt time provides Design and Engineering with pace, rhythm, and a feel for demand—just as it does in production. Andy illustrated how understanding Design Takt helps us level the workload, identify bottlenecks, and focus kaizen thereby. Most launches had fairly predictable resource profile. The key was to make the big picture visible and balance Design resource needs. See Figure 9.6.

TAKT TIME IN DESIGN

Takt time = Operating time ÷ Demand

Suppose demand for various designs in a given five-year period is as follows:

New model launches — 2

Major model changes — 3

Model refresh — 8

What is Takt?

Overall Takt = 60 months/(13) $\sim$ 4.6 months

New model Takt = 60/2 = 30 months

Major model change Takt = 60/3 = 20 months

Model refresh Takt = 60/8 = 7.5 months

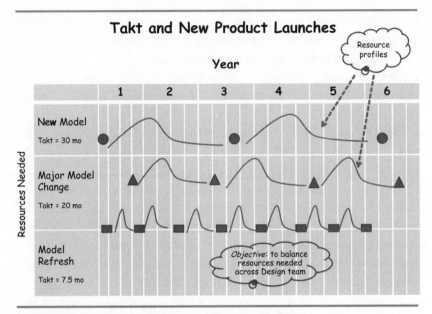

FIGURE 9.6   Takt and New Product Launches

Andy then talked about production physics. He emphasized Little's Law, and the laws of Variability and Variability Buffering. We *wanted* variation in Design, but *not* in the supporting processes (engine test, prototype build, review meetings, and so on). Designers are like jazz musicians—you want them to *play*. But solid standards enable play. For example, standards for changeover and maintenance in the engine test lab liberate the engine designer, who needn't worry about late or incorrect test results. It was good stuff. Here are my summary notes. See Figure 9.7.

We buffer variation with some combination of capacity, lead time, and inventory. In Design, buffering with *capacity* means more people or lots of overtime. Cross-training is a low-cost way of building capacity. It's also useful to have flexible external resources that you can pull in as required. Lean companies have pools of Design technicians trained in core skills for this purpose.

Buffering with *lead time* means delaying launches—unthinkable for Chloe. Buffering with inventory means throwing more projects into the hopper in the hopes something will work—also unthinkable. Chloe has to succeed.

Production Physics—Implications for Design

- Lead time is proportional to Work in Process. Therefore, before you add a project to the hopper, screen it carefully!

- Lead time is inversely proportional to capacity. Therefore, create capacity by cross-training your design and engineering team members.

- In Design, capacity and lead time are the most commonly available buffers. Don't sacrifice lead time! Delay in design means delay in revenue. Buffer with capacity instead.

- Build capacity through cross-training. Enable cross-training by standardizing your core processes so it's easy to plug in new team members.

- Don't overload designers and engineers. Loading them beyond 80% or so means lead times will explode. Buffer the inevitable variation with ''white space'' (open time).

FIGURE 9.7   Production Physics—Implications for Design

PRODUCTION PHYSICS

Little's Law applies in all processes and is the equivalent of Force = Mass $\times$ Acceleration in general physics.

Little's Law: Cycle Time = Work in Process (WIP) $\div$ Throughput, or Throughput = Work in Process (WIP) $\div$ Cycle Time

Definitions:

- Throughput is average output of a process per unit time (e.g., engine tests per day).

- Cycle time for a given routing is the average time from release of the part or unit of work to its arrival at the end of the routing (e.g., the time it takes for an engine to enter, be tested, and leave the test lab).

- Work in process is the inventory accumulated between the start and end points of a routing (e.g., the number of engines in the lab).

Implications:

- For a fixed capacity process, cycle time and WIP are proportional.

- To increase throughput, we can flood our workplace with WIP (the mass production approach); or we can reduce cycle time by reducing waste (Lean approach).

(continued)

(continued)

Related Laws:

- Law of Variability: Increasing variability always increases average cycle times and WIP levels.
- Law of Variability Buffering: Variability in a production system will be buffered by some combination of inventory, capacity, and lead time.
- Law of Capacity Utilization: If a system increases utilization without making other changes, average cycle time will increase in a highly non-linear manner.

Source: Wallace Hopp and Mark Spearman, Factory Physics (New York: McGraw-Hill, 2000).

MUDA, MURA, AND MURI—THE THREE Ms

Muda (waste) is the best known of the Three Ms. *Mura*, which means unevenness or variation, is less known but just as important. W. Edwards Deming, the great American quality sensei, dedicated his life to understanding variation and its corrosive effects.

Muri means "hard to do" and is usually caused by muda and mura. For example, poor ergonomics in a prototype shop (motion waste) inevitably leads to muri. Similarly, widely varying workloads in a design studio (mura) make it difficult for designers to plan and complete work.

Reducing muda, mura, and muri so as to enable flow and pull are cornerstones of Lean improvement activity.

Because variation was inevitable in a new model launch, we needed to use buffers wisely. Andy advised us to buffer with *capacity*. We'd have to build spare capacity internally—through cross-training. Standardization would be a core enabler—standardized processes are easier to teach and backfill.

"Saito-san, how do we create *pull* in Design?" Kurt asked.

We create pull, Andy explained, by defining a small number of "target events" or key milestones, then rigorously reinforcing target event timing and quality. Target events might include chassis and body freeze, styling approval, preliminary prototype builds, full prototype builds, and manufacturing trials.

Target events:

- Take place in the gemba (test site, lab, factory).
- Involve relevant groups (Design, Engineering, Marketing, Manufacturing), including technical experts and senior managers.
- Review physical objects, not just data.
- Focus on creating and sharing knowledge.
- Answer key questions:
  - Do we have a good plan?
  - Do we understand possible alternatives?
  - Does the part or system work as intended?
  - Can we build it?

Reinforcing target event quality and timing depends on leadership and culture, Andy explained. We have to establish and enforce a clear policy that developers *immediately report* anything that might force them to miss a date. Delay is the killer in Design, and much more damaging than, say, missing a cost target. Delay means launch delay—which means we don't get paid.

Knowing they're accountable for meeting target event timing, developers will *pull* for information (engineering drawings, test results, etc.) in the right quantity. This also compels Design and Engineering to develop necessary capacity buffers.

Sam, Kurt, and I absorbed the lesson in silence. I sensed we were touching the surface of a deep pool of knowledge and experience. Andy was giving us what he felt we could absorb. Fixing the big design process would take years and a change in our basic thinking. Improving the small process through Lean basics like visual management and focused kaizen were a necessary bridge. They'd improve problem consciousness, reduce variation, and build our muscles for the big process work ahead. Executive development and the Lean Coordinator Network were also necessary enablers. I was confident that our overall transformation approach was sound.

Harry called me later that day, as I was driving to Detroit Metro Airport. An early Michigan snowstorm had made Hwy 95 slippery. "Tom, I'm taking Dad into Mount Sinai. His blood pressure's a little high and he's not feeling well. Just a precaution; nothing to worry about."

I got on the plane feeling uneasy. When I arrived at LaGuardia, I called Harry again. "Looks like he's okay," Harry said. "They're keeping him overnight as a precaution. The doctor said they might give him a heparin injection later."

"What's heparin?"

"An anticoagulant—it helps prevent blood clots."

IMPLEMENTATION CHECKLIST

1. Understand value and waste in Design and Engineering.
2. Understand the barriers to the flow and absorption of knowledge and implement countermeasures.
3. Develop and implement a yokoten strategy for Design and Engineering.
4. Emphasize flow and the drip, drip, drip (small batch) approach. Learn through rapid experimentation and cheap, quick prototypes. Share learning with frequent, concise status reviews.
5. Understand production physics and its implications for Design and Engineering.
6. Work on the small process and the big process. Learn by doing the former, in preparation for the latter.
7. Ask Designers to seek multiple solutions to design problems. Keep the "cement" fluid as long as possible and converge toward the customer sweet spot.

STUDY QUESTIONS

1. Give at least three examples of knowledge waste in Design and Engineering.
2. From your experience, give at least one example of barriers to
   a. Flow of knowledge
   b. Absorption of knowledge

What are some possible countermeasures?

3. Give at least one example of Little's Law (e.g., time needed to get through a toll booth is proportional to the number of cars in line).

4. Capacity, lead time, and inventory are the three ways we buffer variation in a process. How do we buffer variation in the following areas:

   a. Emergency services (e.g., firefighting)

   b. Organ transplants

   c. NFL quarterbacks

5. How does a typical urban highway illustrate the Law of Capacity Utilization? (For example, compare what happens at rush hour and at 3:00 AM. Any insights?)

6. Assess your organization's design process.

   a. Strengths

   b. Weaknesses

   c. Possible improvements

Chapter 10 Nick Papas Falls into the Abyss

Sarah woke me in the middle of the night. "It's your dad. Harry says come to the hospital at once."

I dressed in a dazed panic. It was early Saturday morning, just past 3:00 AM. Sarah would stay in the apartment with the children. I got into my car, sped through the Lincoln Tunnel, across Manhattan and into Queens. It was lightly snowing and the streets were slippery. I could hear my dad's voice. "Go slow to go fast, my boy . . ."

Harry summarized the situation as I drove. Dad had fallen into a coma. His vital signs were at dangerously low levels. A night-shift nurse found him and initiated emergency response. It was a question of time. If Dad could hang on for the next 24 hours, he would live. With luck, he would avoid brain damage.

I turned left on 21st and headed to Mount Sinai hospital. I parked and sprinted into Emergency. They directed me to the intensive care unit. I found the room.

Dad was unconscious and deathly pale. Tubes were coming out of his arms and his nose. Harry sat next to the bed with his arm around Mama. She was swaying back and forth, saying something in Greek. Her eyes were red.

I leaned in and caressed my father's face. "We're all here, Dad. You're going to be okay."

I kissed my mother and murmured encouragements. Harry and I left the room so we could talk. "What have they done to him?" I asked.

Harry collected himself. "Dad's in a diabetic coma. There was an MAE—a medication administration error—they gave him insulin instead of heparin. His blood sugar and all his vital signs have dropped—it's called *hypoglycemia*. The muscles, the brain can't function . . ."

Harry paused, gathered himself. "The treatment is straightforward—replace the glucose. That's what's in these bags. Dad complained of dizziness, then passed out. We're lucky—because he's a cardiac patient they were monitoring his condition. The night nurse caught it and acted quickly. We'll know in a day or so."

I slumped into a chair. *We might lose him.* My brother sat down next to me. After a few minutes, I spoke. "This is a well-known mistake. It's been all over the news. How could it happen again?"

Harry's face was haggard. "I don't think they're capable of learning."

Hours passed; the sun came up. Mama sat in the chair holding Dad's hand and talking to him. An ever-changing array of doctors and nurses fluttered in and out. I gave Sarah an update and asked her to stay with the children. Teal had left an anxious message. She was in the country with her parents and would return as soon as possible. Their prayers were with us.

I got up and walked around the ICU. The garbage bins were overflowing—in an ICU that emphasized the importance of sterility. Why were the rooms so cheerless and uncomfortable? Why the bizarre schedules that hinder consistency of care? Why the absence of visual management in a place where a misread vial could cause someone's death? Why so little evidence of standards, connections, pathways, and improvement?

A hundred thousand Americans die of medical error every year, Sam Sparrow had estimated—more than double the number of Americans killed in highway accidents, 10 times the number killed in homicides, 20 times the number of our armed forces killed in Iraq and Afghanistan. This does *not* include the equal number taken by hospital-acquired infections.

The data is numbing, incomprehensible—until it becomes personal, until the victim has a face. I remembered the Accident Ratio Pyramid, a cornerstone of safety theory. For every fatality, there is a growing ratio of injuries, close calls, and mistakes. Fatalities are merely the crest of an ocean of hospital-induced misery. Given their management processes, how could it be otherwise? I thought of the hundreds of procedures, medications, and treatments administered each day at Mount Sinai—and shuddered. Sam Sparrow was right—going to the hospital is the most dangerous thing we do. See Figure 10.1.

Why do we tolerate the carnage in our hospitals? A *single* illness from a suspect hamburger can shut down the Humpty Dumpty. I remembered an article I'd read that profiled the efforts of Dr. Paul Probert to reduce the incidence of fatal hospital-borne infections.

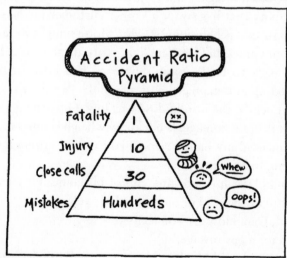

FIGURE 10.1 Accident Ratio Pyramid

Probert's solution? A simple checklist of ICU practices around physician hand-washing and other basic sterilization methods. Hospitals applying Probert's checklist had met with quick success, sharply reducing infection rates within a few months of adoption.

But many physicians rejected the checklist as an unnecessary and insulting bureaucratic intrusion. Hospital administrators were reluctant to push the issue. How is it possible that Dr. Probert had to beg hospitals to adopt an essentially cost-free idea that could save so many lives?

I watched a shift start, a critical connection point. *How many patients in the ward today? What's their status? Who is the case leader? What are the hot spots and watch outs? What critical procedures are we doing today?* I saw nothing that suggested a good hand-off. Things seemed vague, foggy. Why would anybody entrust his or her loved ones to such a process?

No doubt attending staff would tell me everything was in the computer. And I could predict the computer would be wrong. *Hard on the problem, easy on the people.* Health-care professionals are almost always caring and competent. I kept reminding myself.

Why were health-care processes so broken? How had this technologically advanced industry missed the revolution in safety, quality, and productivity that has swept all other customer-facing industries during the past two generations? Taylor Motors might be lagging behind Lean companies, but we were light years ahead of U.S. hospitals.

I walked back to Dad's room. Someone had brought breakfast. Harry looked up and managed a weary smile. "Dad's vital signs are improving. Luckily, the insulin dose was low. Only thing we have to worry about is brain damage. We'll know when he comes to."

Mama squeezed my hand. "Don't you worry, chriso mou. Your father is going to be okay."

A few hours later my dad came out of his coma. He tried to grin. "How are you my boy?" For once he wasn't yelling.

"I'm good, Dad. How are you feeling?"

"Not bad for a guy my age."

"Listen to him," said Mama. "He's making jokes. Please call everybody and tell them Nicky's going to be okay."

Dad stayed in the hospital for a few more days. Get well cards, flowers, and Greek pastries poured in. Humpty Dumpty customers chipped in for Rangers tickets and a basket of fresh fruit. Within a week Dad was back at work, part-time. We'd see how things went in the New Year. Uncle Angie and Aunt Toula would keep the Humpty Dumpty going in the interim.

But we had unfinished business with the hospital. A medication error had nearly caused a family catastrophe. At Taylor Motors serious safety incidents trigger detailed investigations, whether there's an injury or not. We know severity is usually a matter of luck. We seek root causes and try to make permanent countermeasures.

So I asked the hospital for *its* accident investigation. I wanted to know root cause and what countermeasures it planned to prevent this from happening again. I got stonewalled. There was no evidence they'd done a formal investigation.

"They'll paper this over," said Harry. "We can take them to court but what good would it do?" He was right. Would it motivate the hospital to get to the root cause? Would it motivate them to improve standards, connections, and pathways, so medication errors became impossible?

Harry put together a likely scenario of what had happened. "Dad was showing signs of cardiac distress. The nurses were anxious to help him. One of them injected Dad with the wrong drug. Both heparin and insulin are clear liquids and are kept in vials that are hard to distinguish. By size, shape, and texture, they have the same feel. The labels are different but the vials are small and the labels even smaller. Often these drugs are stored close to one another. Imagine a tired nurse at midnight after a 10-hour shift, anxious to help a patient in distress. It's easy to make a mistake in the circumstances."

Hard on the problem, easy on the people. The problem is almost always the system—not the person. Most people want to do a good job. Sam Sparrow's image of the deep, complex, and disconnected silos came to mind.

"The nurse was tricked, Harry, by packaging, presentation, lighting . . . Andy says people are animals who make mistakes. We're not hardwired for absolute reliability. That's why we need standardized work and defect proofing. To make it easy to do the right thing—and hard to do the wrong thing.

"The system failed the nurse, as it failed Dad," I went on. "The system's parts—doctors, nurses, pharmacists—and corresponding hierarchies—failed to work together. I'll bet the medication administration process has no owner."

Harry nodded. "That's why there's so little learning. Nobody looks across the disconnected silos. So hospital workers scramble in the dark, hoping to avoid catastrophe."

Ignorant armies clashing by night . . .

"What are the core mental models in health care?" I asked.

Harry was familiar with our NJMM work. "Here's the most basic mental model. There are *three* parties involved: the *patient*, *provider* (i.e., the hospital), and the *payer* (i.e., the insurer). As you can imagine, this leads to confusion.

"Hospitals *say* they put the patient first—but the *payer* pays the bills. Now the patient and payer have different objectives. The patient wants to stay healthy at reasonable cost. The payer wants to keep costs down and provide good returns for shareholders. These sound similar—but are not."

"So the patient is *not* the arbiter of value," I put in. "Is that why you can't get a straight answer on cost or quality?"

Harry nodded. "Some hospitals actively discourage their people from giving out cost or quality info."

It made sense. If the patient isn't your customer, why give them any info? "Harry, how are *problems* viewed in health care?"

"Problems are garbage to be hidden or ignored," Harry replied. "Making problems visible is unthinkable—they're afraid of lawsuits. Stop and fix, like you do in manufacturing, is also unthinkable. People work around problems."

"How are *leaders* viewed in health care?" I asked. "Are they bosses or senseis?"

"In health care, leaders tell people what to do," Harry answered. "Doctors run hospitals for themselves. It's not done with malice. It's just the way it's always been."

"How about hospital standards? Do they entail content, sequence, timing, and expected outcome? Are there embedded tests to make problems visible?"

Harry smiled. "You're joking with me, right? Where standards exist, they're typically complex, hard-to-understand and handed down from on high. Simple, visual one-pagers, developed by the users, and comprising the elements you mentioned are rare in most hospitals."

How could it be otherwise? "How about the scientific method? Do health-care practitioners practice PDCA?"

"Each individual discipline has its own version of PDCA, which they practice reasonably well in their silos. But they don't practice PDCA *across* silos—for the reasons we've discussed. Nobody can see the entire value stream. Nobody owns the entire process.

"By the way," Harry went on, "when I said 'they're incapable of learning,' I meant the hospital system—not the people. Health-care workers tend to be smart and capable. I think they'd pick up your Lean approach very quickly. But the system works against learning."

I made a mental note, in case Andy and I ever did start a consulting company. "How about 'customer-in' mentality?"

Harry shook his head. "As we've established, the payer—not the patient—is the customer."

"So who almost killed our Dad?" I asked. "Was it the nurse, pharmacist, doctor? No, Harry, it was the lousy management system—the interactions between silos."

"And lousy mental models," Harry added.

The implications were clear. System management was a separate discipline. Hospitals, like Taylor Motors, require Shusas, who "wrap their arms around" critical value streams. Hospitals would benefit from the three-pronged approach we'd adopted in the Chloe platform: executive development, Lean Coordinator Network, and focused improvement activities. These would begin to connect the silos, and change core mental models within them.

Still, I didn't feel we were at the root cause. I showed Harry my first cut at problem solving our health-care mess. Root cause: *The patient is not the customer—the insurer is*. Thus, the patient is *not* the arbiter of value. Waste and value inevitably become muddled. Result: hospital-inflicted carnage at crippling, unsustainable expense.

Therefore, a guiding principle of any health-care reform would be to put the patient—the true customer—at the center of the system. Nobody can allocate health-care dollars better than the patient. Nobody can better drive quality, delivery, and cost improvement. Government and insurers clearly can't. In fact, no centralized reimbursement system is supple enough to address all the variables affecting the patient's experience. Only the patient, like the customer in any free-market economy, can be relied on to make the subtle, dynamic buying decisions that compel innovation.

I wished the current administration well, but saw little in their proposed reforms that addressed root cause. Nor did I see a solution in the Canadian single payer model. It, too, failed to address the root cause. My Toronto cousins had their own horror stories and Canadian health-care costs were spiking.

TOM'S FOUR-STEP PROBLEM SOLVING

1. Do we have a problem? Yes. Nick Papas fell into a hypoglycemic coma after being mismedicated.
2. Do we know the cause?

   Point of Cause: The moment the night nurse detected Dad's plummeting blood sugar levels.

   Direct Cause: A hospital staff member injected Dad with the insulin.

   Root Cause: Do Six Why analysis.

   > Why did staff member inject Nick with insulin instead of heparin? Because he or she could.
   >
   > Why? Because the heparin and insulin are stored close to one another in nearly identical vials with small, barely legible labels.
   >
   > Why? Because there is no standard requiring that they not be stored in this way.
   >
   > Why? Because it's not important to the hospital.
   >
   > Why? Because it's not important to the hospital's customer.
   >
   > Why? Because the customer, (Medicare, the insurer), is not personally affected by such errors. The insurer simply passes the cost onto the payer (the government, in this case).

   Root Cause: The patient is not the customer, (the insurer is).

   Countermeasure: Make the patient the customer.
3. Have I confirmed cause and effect?

   What experiments might we run?
4. Have I confirmed the countermeasure?

How to put the patient at the center of the system? My head began doing a double-time rumba. We need insurance coverage for two kinds of health risk: noncatastrophic and catastrophic. Non-catastrophic means routine care like annual physicals, and treatment for minor injuries and illness. Catastrophic illness would mean illnesses exceeding a threshold of, say $50,000.

What if each citizen contributed to a personal, tax-deferred health-care fund—a 401(k) for health, if you will? All Americans would be required to buy it and it would provide insurance against *catastrophic* illness. For noncatastrophic risk, every American would also be required to contribute to an insurance vehicle similar to the current Health Savings Account (HSA). People would pay for noncatastrophic health care directly from their HSAs. Catastrophic illness would be handled by their health-care 401(k). For lower income people who couldn't afford the premiums, government would fill the gap.

What about expenses that fell through the cracks—major expenses that weren't large enough to qualify for catastrophic insurance but still exceeded the amount in a person's HSA? Examples might include a birth, sports injury, or appendectomy. We'd handle these with *credit*. You'd be allowed to borrow against future contributions to your HSA to cover major health needs.

A few weeks later Sam Sparrow and I had our regular monthly phone call. Sam had visited CMM several times. Sarah and I had taken him to Yankee Stadium. Now it was hockey season, and Sam loved the Bruins almost as much as the Red Sox. I was trying to get us tickets to the upcoming Rangers-Bruins game.

I told Sam about my Dad's experience. He commiserated and said he wasn't surprised. I shared my brainwave, knowing health care was his focus.

"Interesting proposal, Tom. A number of people have come to the same conclusion about root cause. And they're proposing counter-measures not dissimilar to yours. The merits are obvious. If people are paying for health care out of their own pockets, we'll see an end to price fog, and to unreadable hospital bills. Doctors would spend less time on insurance-related paperwork, and more time with the customer.

"Most important of all, we'd see an end to the current 'use it or lose it' mind-set. Our current model encourages 'moral hazard'—people keep spending money because they believe *somebody else* is paying for it. But, as we're learning, there is nobody else."

"Any chance these ideas will take root, Sam?"

Sam nodded. "It's called customer-centered health care, and it's *starting* to take root. Just a few shoots, but encouraging nonetheless. Some retailers, for example, are rolling out retail clinics for routine care like physicals, blood work, and common treatments like cold and flu. But moving to a customer-centered system will take a long time, and it'll be complicated."

"What can we do in the interim?"

"The administration is focused on the insurer and wants to make insurance less restrictive and less costly. They also want to provide a public option to increase competition. So the current debate is about health *insurance*—not health care.

"On the provider side, we can improve safety, quality, and productivity—through the kind of work you're doing at Taylor Motors. Tom, I'm not sure you realize how powerful your approach would be in health care. Finally, patients have a responsibility to take better care of themselves."

"We're still not at root cause, Sam."

Sam nodded again. "They say politics is the art of the possible."

"I wanted to ask you about learning. As we've discussed, Chloe's success hinges on shared, experiential learning. My brother Harry said something troubling about hospitals. He said they were *in-capable* of learning. Is he right? If so, how do we increase learning velocity in a hospital, or any organization?"

"That's the focus of my work these days. Short answer to your first question: *Yes*, most hospitals as currently structured are not good at learning—or at sharing learning. Learning and problem solving are inextricably linked. Why do we learn, if not to solve problems and make our lives better? Four capabilities underlie learning. I call them C1, C2, C3, and C4:

- C1: Design standards such that they make problems visible.
- C2: Stop and fix problems made visible.
- C3: Share the learning laterally (yokoten).
- C4: Leaders develop people, and, in particular, their ability to solve problems.

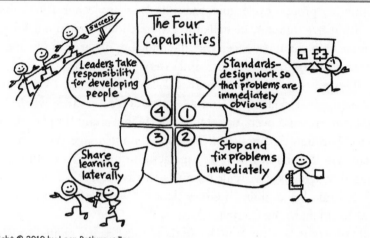

FIGURE 10.2   The Four Capabilities

I drew it out as he spoke.[1] See Figure 10.2.

"They're related to the Four Rules, of course," Sam continued. "C1 is about making problems visible and is related to Rules 1, 2, and 3. The purpose of self-diagnostic *standards, connections,* and *pathways* is, after all, to make problems visible. Remember the spider web metaphor? We want to know what filaments are breaking as soon as possible. That's why we have tests.

"C2 entails a help chain—a form of connection between management levels that ensures the problem gets fixed as soon as possible. This is a tough one for managers. They often resent being called to a line or process stoppage because they think *their* work is more important. Truth is, nothing is more important than stopping and fixing the problem—so the process can get going again. Extending the spider web metaphor, if the junior spider can't repair the filament, he calls for a more senior spider. But the filament has to get fixed no matter what."

"Makes sense," I said. "Our help chain at NJMM connects all the way to the plant manager. If the team member can't fix the problem

---

[1] These ideas are informed and inspired by the work of my friend and colleague, Dr. Steven Spear. For a deeper discussion of the Four Capabilities, I recommend Dr. Spear's recent book, *Chasing the Rabbit* (New York: McGraw-Hill, 2009).

within her process cycle time, she calls the team leader. If he can't fix it within five minutes, he calls the group leader, and so on. We have similar help chains between the line and support groups like maintenance, engineering, and health and safety."

"Those are good examples of C2," Sam went on. "C3 is about yokoten—shared lateral learning—so we don't have to solve the same problem over and over. Yokoten is hugely important for big organizations. Through yokoten, *scale becomes an advantage.* You can apply what you learned in Brazil to your activities in China or India. I repeat, through yokoten, scale becomes an advantage!"

My brain began doing a Greek dance. "Wonderful, Sam! Yokoten is an antidote to Big Company Disease!"

"You got it, amigo. Now let's talk about C4. It's related to Rule 4 (Improvement) and to your 'Leader equals sensei' mental model. If we accept the centrality of problem solving and yokoten, the leader's Job One is developing people."

"*See a problem, solve a problem, share what you've learned,*" I said, "the remedy to Big Company Disease. And the leader's role is to ensure people are seeing, solving, and sharing—across the organization." See Figure 10.3.

FIGURE 10.3   The Remedy to Big Company Disease

"Bingo," Sam Sparrow said.

"One more question, Sam. How do we apply the remedy *outside* Taylor Motors—in our supply chain?"

Sam took a deep breath. "Whoa, that's a big question."

IMPLEMENTATION CHECKLIST

1. Develop standards that make problems visible quickly.
2. Create ownership by involving team members in the development of standards.
3. Develop "help chains" in your organization so that you "stop and fix" problems immediately.
4. Develop and implement a strategy for shared, experiential learning (yokoten).
5. Amend job descriptions so that leaders are explicitly responsible for developing the capability of their people.

STUDY QUESTIONS

1. Tom says the problem is "almost always in the system." What does he mean?

   a. Give three examples from your own experience.

2. What would content, sequence, timing, and expected outcome look like for a hospital pharmacy process? What embedded tests might such a process include (e.g., am I using the right container, right label size, and color)?

3. What would a direct, binary, self-diagnostic connection between a hospital pharmacy and an ICU look like (e.g., clearly defined points of contact, clear standards for cycle time, other)?

4. How might we make a shift change in a hospital ICU direct, binary, and self-diagnostic?

5. Give three examples each of value and waste for a health-care insurer.

6. Give three examples each of value and waste for a patient.

7. In what ways are insurer and patient value similar? In what ways are they different?

8. Give at least one example of each of the Four Capabilities from your experience.
9. Assess the Four Capabilities in your organization.
    a. How might you improve the Four Capabilities in your zone of control?

Chapter 11   My Beautiful Mind— Leaning Out Our Supply Chain

It was late January and the trees were glazed with ice. The glow of Christmas had subsided and we settled in for a few more months of winter. My relationship with my ex-wife continued to improve. Teal and I had become a team committed to raising our daughters together. Sophie and Helen sensed the change and were happy. Teal had joined an Internet dating service and had some prospects. I was pleased for her.

Sarah and I were getting along as well as ever. Over the holidays we took the kids to see the Nutcracker ballet at Lincoln Center, Sarah pointing out the famous Chagall tapestries. We went skating at Rockefeller Center, saw Santa at Macy's, and took in Fifth Avenue's glorious shop windows. "Sarah is a great girl," Harry told me. "You should snap her up."

I agreed with him. Should I wait until after Chloe's launch, I wondered?

Chloe was on track. Plans were clear, problems visible, and team members engaged. We were applying our transformation plan effectively. Focused kaizen and the Lean Coordinator Network had spread across the value stream—at differing rates, but that was normal. Another wave of executive development had begun. Chloe's design team had come up with elegant and inexpensive improvements that lined up well with our True North. Obeyas had blossomed across the platform and had improved problem solving and decision making. Barring the unforeseen, Chloe would launch on time, on budget, and with quality.

Art Juna's commercials were creating a buzz around Chloe—and around Taylor Motors. We'd started paying off our federal loans early and expected to be free and clear by year-end. Some people questioned whether we were being too aggressive.

I haven't talked much about our activities in manufacturing—it wasn't our constraint. Connecticut Motor Manufacturing (CMM) was on schedule for Chloe's May 1 launch. The on-site pilot center allowed team members to play with tools and equipment and develop effective standardized work in advance. CMM's proximity to NJMM was a bonus. There was much yokoten between factories.

Stand-up checking in the CMM obeya accelerated as we neared launch. What began as a weekly one-hour check was now a daily 9:00 AM check. The obeya's four walls reflected CMM's focus areas: People, Quality, Delivery, and Cost. Key thinkers reported out hot spots and coordinated countermeasure plans.

I had no illusions. Transforming an entire platform would take several years. At best, we would partially succeed. But even partial success would make us stand out like a wart on a bald head.

Morgan and May had been strangely quiet the past few months. Something was coming.

"What does *partner* mean, Becky-san?"

Becky, Andy, and I were doing a waste walk at Champion Trim, one of Chloe's most important suppliers. We were starting in the shipping department and would give the plant manager, Ken Boldin, a summary and suggestions. Ken was caught in traffic and would join us when he arrived. Ken enjoyed our gemba walks and always took plenty of notes.

Becky was our point person on supply chain and had been reaching out to critical suppliers. Our intent was to help them by offering executive development and focused kaizen activities—gratis. We would also help them set up their Lean Coordinator Network. The supplier would keep all savings generated through kaizen for the first six months. Thereafter, we'd split the savings.

Supply chain is a monster, and one of our biggest challenges. Joe Jacobsen and Purchasing have treated suppliers badly for a long time. Yet we can't succeed without them. It'll be a long road back.

"*Partner* means trust, friendship, and shared goals," Becky replied. "It means you break bread together and look out for one another."

We were in the staging area. Andy was checking this hour's shipments. Becky and I were doing a quick count of finished goods inventory. "Why should we look on suppliers as partners?" Andy asked.

"Because suppliers represent 75 percent of our cost," Becky answered. "We have a shared path. Either we succeed together—or we fail together. I've done all the homework you gave us. Turns out treating suppliers right is not just good ethics, it's also good business."

"Please explain, Becky-san."

"It's a Nash equilibrium. Did ya'll see that Russell Crowe movie called *A Beautiful Mind*? It's about John Nash, the mathematician and Nobel Prize winner, and how brilliant he was, and how he lost his mind and everything."

"Good movie," I said. "What's it got to do with how we treat suppliers?"

"John Nash studied game theory. A Nash equilibrium exists when two parties know each other's strategy, and *cannot* do better by changing their strategies. So it's best to keep doing what you're doing."

"I'm not sure I follow, Becky."

"If we and our suppliers *cooperate* and share ideas on improving safety, quality, and cost, the pie gets bigger and we all win. Everybody benefits by staying the course, so it's a Nash equilibrium. If we don't cooperate, the pie gets smaller, and we all lose."

Becky walked over to a flip chart outside the conveyance team room. "Let me draw it out." See Figure 11.1.

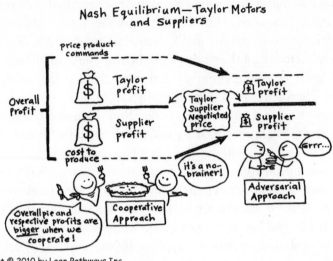

FIGURE 11.1   Nash Equilibrium—Taylor Motors and Suppliers

"If we cooperate," Becky summarized, "everybody wins. Suppliers get a long-term contract, fair price, steady demand, and far less paperwork through EDI. We get better quality and lead time, lower cost and less risk of being shut down by part shortages."

That's why we begin business meetings with a handshake, I thought. It's an expression of trust and a commitment to a mutual standard of behavior. "And if somebody cheats, they lose out," I added.

Becky nodded. "They may benefit in the short term. But the other party soon recognizes they've been double-crossed. They quickly change to an adversarial strategy—and everybody loses. The rational strategy is 'Tit for Tat.' We cooperate unless provoked. If provoked, we retaliate. But we're quick to forgive if the other party changes to a cooperative strategy."

"Does cooperation mean we become *soft*?" I asked. "You know, we join hands with suppliers and sing camp songs?"

Becky shook her head. "Course not. We're demanding with our suppliers, and we're tough negotiators. But we keep the big picture in mind. We don't burn the furniture."

"We've been burning furniture for a long time," I said. "We're reaching out to our suppliers now. How are they reacting?"

"Chloe suppliers are beginning to trust *us*—but they don't trust Joe Jacobsen. Champion Trim is one of the few that's opening the kimono, and that's only because they know Rachel's running interference."

"It will take a long time," said Andy. "But we must create mutual trust with suppliers."

It would take time, indeed. I was struck, again, by Toyota's intuitive grasp of a fundamental principle—one we'd failed to grasp, at great cost. They were a brilliant company indeed. As Sam Sparrow suggested, they could well come back stronger than ever.

We walked over to the forklift parking lot. Andy checked the condition of parked trucks. I reviewed posted maintenance records. Becky checked safety standards at the battery charging station. "Becky-san," Andy went on, "what are common mental models in supply chain division?"

"Our planners are taught Economic Order Quantity in school," Becky replied. "The idea is that there's an optimal batch size. It's not wrong; in fact it can be helpful. But EOQ is limiting, because it's *static*. EOQ assumes ordering and storage costs are fixed—but they aren't. Through kaizen we can continually reduce these costs. That's the key with Lean—the workplace is a *control point*. Nothing is fixed, nothing is 'given.' And here's the critical point: *batch size determines cost structure*."

"Please explain, Becky-san."

"Big batches mean you have to scale up—more machines, more loading and receiving docks, more forklifts and tractor trailers, more warehouses and distribution centers, more supply chain specialists tracking all the extra stuff, more software to track everything . . ."

"It's like trying to suck a tennis ball through a garden hose," I put in. "We have to buy a bigger hose and a bigger pump. It's odd that we're addicted to big batches. At home, do we buy 20 heads of lettuce at a time? Of course not; we buy in small batches. Otherwise, we'd have to buy a bigger fridge and eat lettuce every day." See Figure 11.2.

"Here's a related mental model," said Becky. "*Get the lowest piece price*. It's gospel for our buyers. So we move production offshore in an endless quest for lowest piece price—because EOQ assumes order and storage costs are fixed. It also assumes lead time is zero, by the way—another fallacy.

"So we create supply chains that look like *spaghetti*: tangled, 10,000-mile pathways full of variation—which we have to buffer

Copyright © 2010 by Lean Pathways Inc.

FIGURE 11.2   Tennis Ball Through a Garden Hose

with inventory, capacity, and lead time. Then we fly in planeloads of engineers and executives each month to fix all the quality and reliability problems. And because the supply chain is so long and twisted, there's *fog* everywhere—which we try to dispel with software so complex no one person understands more than a few screens. And that's all supposed to be *cheaper,* so we lay off thousands of people stateside . . ."

I smiled. "You're passionate about this!"

"I don't want to be misunderstood," she said. "If demand is very stable and it's a commodity product with few design changes, it could make sense to source in the lowest cost region. But if demand is variable, and if the product is specialized, we should source locally. You have to think it through. Every part has a story."

Andy nodded. "Every part, product, line, factory, and value stream has a story."

We walked from shipping into the production area. Ken Boldin was waiting for us. We exchanged greetings and I summarized our walk to that point. Injection molding machines were cycling all around us. I was impressed with Ken's noise-reduction work. We didn't need earplugs.

"Becky, any other common mental models in supply chain planning?" I asked.

"Production schedules *change all the time*," Becky answered. "We're always looking to 'optimize' by shifting production between facilities and suppliers. Our planners have sophisticated software that finds the 'best solution.'"

I nodded. "I call it the 'digitization fallacy'—the idea that software will save us from bad processes."

"Well, all these schedule changes kill us—and our suppliers," Becky said. "By the way, we also have software to optimize inventory. Result: Tractor trailers full of parts ping-pong randomly around the continent."

"Are connections direct, binary, and self-diagnostic?" I asked, knowing the answer. "Are pathways simple, prespecified, and a diagnostic?"

Becky shook her head. "Our connections are random and confusing. Our pathways look like spaghetti. Again, I don't want to be misunderstood. Our planners want to do the right thing. They just don't know any better. It's all a computer game to them."

"My Uncle Angie has a saying," I said. "*Nowadays, you can crap at the speed of light.*"

Andy smiled. "What is wrong with constant schedule changes, Ken-san?"

"You never know what you're going to make," Ken replied. "You never develop a rhythm—you just react. It's hard to get better . . ."

"Have ya'll seen the movie *Groundhog Day*?" Becky asked. "Bill Murray is this self-centered jerk who has to relive the same day over and over again. He wants to get to know Andie McDowell better, but she can't stand him.

"Because Bill gets to live the same day over and over, he *learns*. He starts helping people out, reading, reflecting, and working on himself. He becomes a better person. When the loop is finally broken, Andie likes the person he's become. Bill ends up getting the girl." See Figure 11.3.[1]

"So we need to provide a Groundhog Day experience for our factories and suppliers," I summed up.

"Sign me up," said Ken.

---

[1] My friend and colleague, Ron Taylor, is the source of this marvelous metaphor.

FIGURE 11.3   Groundhog Day

Andy walked over to the asaichi[2] table to examine the previous day's defects. Champion Trim was piloting asaichi, with our help. "How can we provide schedule stability?" Andy asked.

"By applying *heijunka*," Becky answered, "which means leveling demand by volume and mix—from the customer all the way upstream. Mr. Saito has been teaching us heijunka and it's amazing. I thought just-in-time meant producing what the customer consumed— but that's not right! In fact, if you do that, you'll likely make things *worse* by transmitting variation all the way upstream. Mr. Saito, could I ask you to explain?"

Andy went to a flip chart by the asaichi table. "Heijunka has three characters: *hei, jun,* and *ka. Hei* means "level," *jun* means "production ratios," and *ka* means "get better every day." See Figure 11.4.[3]

"If we produce to customer demand, which varies day to day, we transmit *mura* into our value stream. Not good!" See Figure 11.5.

---

[2] *Asaichi* means "morning market" in Japanese and entails reviewing the previous day's most important quality defects and doing on-the-spot problem solving.

[3] I'm obliged to Ron Taylor for these and other insights into heijunka. Many of them are based on his many presentations at Lean Pathways conferences over the years. Thanks, sensei.

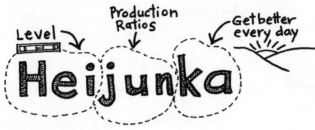

FIGURE 11.4   Heijunka

"Instead, planning and scheduling teams must provide a leveled pro-duction schedule," Andy went on, "and leveled *information flows*."

At NJMM Andy taught us that Planning's product was information and that their customer was Production. People did what their in-formation told them to do. If the info was wrong, they'd do the

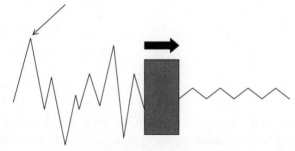

FIGURE 11.5   Produce to a Fluctuating Order? No! Produce to Leveled Demand
Source: "Heijunka," by Ron Taylor, Lean Pathways Fall Conference, Toronto, November 2009.

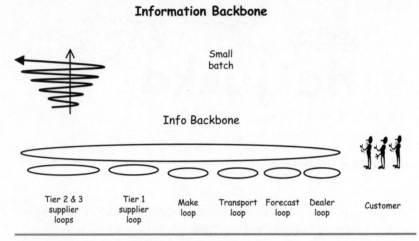

Information Backbone

Small batch

Info Backbone

Tier 2 & 3 supplier loops | Tier 1 supplier loop | Make loop | Transport loop | Forecast loop | Dealer loop | Customer

FIGURE 11.6 Information Backbone
Source: "Heijunka," by Ron Taylor, Lean Pathways Fall Conference, Toronto, November 2009.

wrong thing. In fact, there was a spine or backbone of information (see Figure 11.6) comprising various loops including:

- Forecasting
- Transportation
- Make
- Tier 1
- Tier 2
- Tier etc.

These information loops connected the various silos and dispelled the fog. Strengthening them entailed business process kaizen. We had to undo the Gordian knot one strand at a time. Five Why analysis inevitably led us to root causes in the management system, such as:

- Stability and/or capability of manpower, machines, methods, or materials.
- Dysfunctional mental models.
- Dysfunctional reward structures.
- Human resources policies, and so forth.

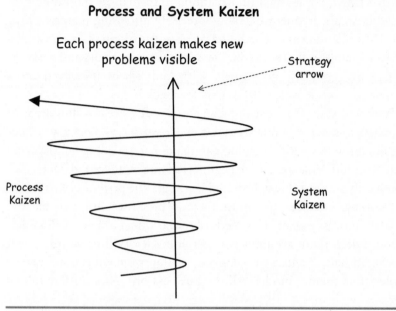

FIGURE 11.7   Process and System Kaizen
Source: "Heijunka," by Ron Taylor, Lean Pathways Fall Conference, Toronto, November 2009.

The helix of improvement, Andy taught us, was never-ending and swung between process and system kaizen. The arrow of strategy deployment provided the overall direction. See Figure 11.7.

Heijunka is amazing, as Becky said. It entails mimicking demand from the customer all the way upstream. Tricky part is, the signal needs to be translated at *each node* in the supply chain. Both production *rates* and *ratios* have to be right. The former requires a good grasp of Takt time, the latter, and a good bill of materials (BOM) process. Some ratios are obvious. One car means one steering wheel and four tires. But others are not and that's where BOM accuracy comes in.

Other important planning processes include inventory accuracy, customer, and item and supplier masters. If core planning processes are broken, you *lose the signal*. Pretty soon you're drifting in fog. You buffer with inventory, capacity, and lead time—and your cost structure balloons.

At NJMM, we learned that planning information should be provided in small, frequent batches—precisely mirroring material flow. NJMM's planning and scheduling process was originally an unwieldy 12-week monster that sucked up hundreds of man-hours and was out-of-date the moment it was issued. With Andy's help, it evolved into a nimble four-week cycle with weekly feedback loops.

With Chloe we were engaging an entire value stream—hundreds of suppliers *upstream*; hundreds of dealers *downstream*. Becky was leading our activities with incoming parts and materials. Elaine Miyazaki and Antonio Villarreal had begun working with our dealers. We could only succeed through shared learning. The prize was worth it.

Planning processes, like most business processes, are invisible and have no process owner. The needs of the customer are not well understood. Often there are multiple customers with differing needs, yet no "handshake." Moreover, continuous improvement is not a widely understood mental model. All the business process stuff I've talked about.

Another important NJMM lesson was that Planning was *not* the enemy. They're often referred to as the "monster"—but half the time the monster doesn't know it's hurting you. They've inherited bad processes and wrong thinking. When the planners realized we weren't blaming them, they relaxed and worked with us.

Now Andy was drawing out traditional scheduling logic: *build to a fixed inventory (or lead time)*. See Figure 11.8.

Andy then illustrated what unleveled demand looks like several days later. See Figure 11.9.

"Within days, each point in the supply chain is making something different, Andy said. "We lose the *feel* for demand."

Kenny gave Andy a hangdog look. "You're describing Champion Trim, Mr. Saito. Never realized the effect till now."

"Before Andy, we were the same at NJMM," I told him. "Each department made different things with little connection to the next process. We had no feel for demand."

Andy then drew out heijunka scheduling logic. "We allow inventory and/or lead time to fluctuate between predetermined min/max levels—and production gets a stable schedule." See Figure 11.10.

"Makes perfect sense," Ken said. "We should buffer customer variability with inventory or lead time."

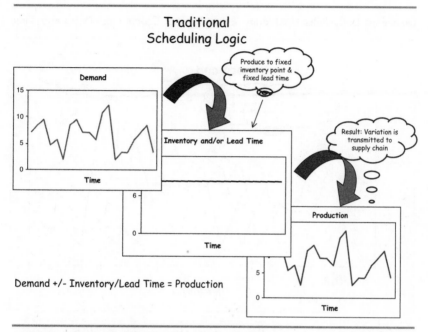

FIGURE 11.8   Traditional Scheduling Logic
Source: "Heijunka," by Ron Taylor, Lean Pathways Fall Conference,
Toronto, November 2009.

"It takes guts," I put in. "You've got to trust the buffers and your
heijunka logic. You can't freak out when a given part is nearing its
minimum level. Just keep building to Takt and you'll be okay."

"Keep building to Takt," Ken repeated, "and let the buffers absorb
the variation."

"How do we mimic demand upstream—in our supply chain?"
Andy asked.

"Through direct, binary connections—good handshakes—between
customers and suppliers," Becky answered. "Suppliers must be able
to *see* what customers are consuming, and whether they're ahead or
behind. We need visible control points to dispel the fog. Ahead/
behind, inventory, lead time, and quality are the main ones."

"How does the bullwhip effect fit in, Becky?" Ken asked.

Becky went to the whiteboard. "When lead times are long and
customer–supplier connections weak, small variations in customer
demand create tidal waves upstream—that's the bullwhip effect.

Unleveled Daily Pulls Upstream—Each Process Equals One-Day Lead Time

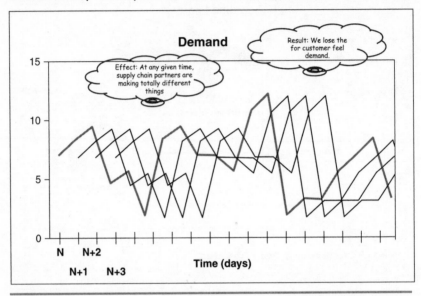

FIGURE 11.9   Unleveled Daily Pulls Upstream—Each Process Equals One-Day Lead Time
Source: "Heijunka," by Ron Taylor, Lean Pathways Fall Conference, Toronto, November 2009.

There's an online supply chain game you can play called the Beer Game,[4] which illustrates it. The Beer Game's underlying assumptions are: Supply chain members do *not* share information, and there are long *delays* between ordering and receiving materials. People try different strategies to minimize cost and maximize customer service. But because of the system weaknesses I mentioned, cost tends to explode."

"So how do we minimize the bullwhip effect, Becky?" I asked.

"All the stuff we've been talking about," she answered. "First, share information up and down the supply chain. Second, cooperate with your supply chain partners on demand and capacity issues.

---

[4] The Beer Game was developed by MIT and is accessible at http://beergame.mit.edu.

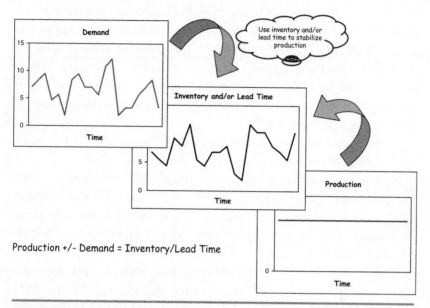

FIGURE 11.10   Heijunka Scheduling Logic
Source: "Heijunka," by Ron Taylor, Lean Pathways Fall Conference, Toronto, November 2009.

Third, reduce lead times—both for materials *and* information. That means lots of business process kaizen.

"Aligned objectives are also critical—a tough nut at Taylor Motors. Except for the Chloe project, our leaders are rewarded for optimizing unit efficiency—not overall efficiency. Nobody owns overall lead time, inventory, and quality. So everybody 'succeeds' and gets their bonus. But the customer—and the company—lose."

"That's what Chloe's all about," I said, "alignment upstream and downstream so the customer can win."

"The Shusa speaks for the customer," Andy summed up. "We need to mimic demand across the platform. Information flow is critical and a big challenge for the reasons discussed."

"Chloe's supply chain kickoff session was certainly different," Kenny said. "Becky, would you mind summarizing your supply chain plan again?"

"There are three phases," Becky replied. "*Stabilize, flow*, and *pull*. Realistically, it'll take three years. We've started with our top 10 suppliers. We're applying our transformation model and the learn-by-do principle. Each supply chain partner has committed to strategy deployment, a Lean Coordinator Network, and executive development.

"*Stabilize* means implement Lean basics. Rules 1 (Standards) and 4 (Problem Solving) are fundamental. You can't pull or flow unless you're stable. Strategy deployment is also a great stabilizer because it focuses and aligns activity."

"People want to jump to flow and pull," I commented, "but without stability you're building a house on quicksand."

"*Flow* means reducing batch sizes and strengthening connections and pathways—Rules 2 and 3," Becky went on. "We typically segment demand in terms of Runners (generally high volume, low variability) and Strangers (generally lower volume and high variability). Then we introduce pattern production so that suppliers can experience the Groundhog Day effect. By cycling through the same patterns, we're hopeful suppliers will start to learn and solve problems. We'll use a proxy for customer demand—our best guess is fine at this point. We'll also introduce control points, as I said: ahead/behind, adherence to schedule, inventory, and lead time."

"*Pull* means heijunka and connecting to the customer. We want to mimic leveled customer demand across our supply chain. We'll adjust our production patterns and control points to leveled demand."

"What are the expected benefits?" Ken asked.

"If we do this right and are lucky," Becky said, "we'll see inventory and scrap reduction first. Lead time and customer service benefits should follow. But the gold ring is cost structure. We do this right, money will fall from the sky."

"I'll wear a hard hat," said Ken, smiling.

It was Saturday morning and Harry and I were having breakfast at the Humpty Dumpty. Dad was back at work five days a week—his upper limit. We were watching him closely. So far, so good—he was sticking with the program Dr. Stratas had given him. Sundays and Mondays off.

Dad spent his days off taking long walks when the weather permitted, doing volunteer work at St. Irene's, and kibitzing with his pals at the Greek-American center. Mama allowed him into the Humpty

Dumpty on days off, but wouldn't let him into the kitchen. It was tough on the old goat. "I just want to make sure everything is shipshape . . ."

I liked the Humpty Dumpty's frowsy winter warmth. The windows were steamy, the air rich with aromas: feta cheese omelets, home fries, coffee . . . Uncle Angie sashayed over to our table. "How are my favorite nephews?"

"Poli kala, theo," I said. "How's the pest control business?"

"Excellent, my boy! Did I tell you the one about the wife, the moth, and the pest-control guy?"

"I think you did," said Harry, wincing.

We chin-wagged a while, then Angie went over to the bar to chat with Uncle Louie. I wanted to talk to Harry about Sarah. "She's a wonderful girl, Harry. It's time to pop the question. But I want it to be special."

"Wonderful news!" said Harry. I reminded him that she hadn't accepted yet. "She will, she will," he assured me. "Now let's get to work on your proposal plan . . ."

A little voice told me I should've kept quiet.

IMPLEMENTATION CHECKLIST

1. Build long-term relationships with suppliers. Understand the Nash Equilibrium and seek shared improvement activities.
2. Recognize the connection between batch size and cost structure. Seek to gradually reduce batch size.
3. Base supply chain decisions on total cost, not piece price.
4. Build direct, binary, self-diagnostic connections with suppliers.
5. Develop simple, prespecified, self-diagnostic pathways with suppliers.
6. Understand and implement heijunka. Recognize the importance of stable schedules and seek to create the Groundhog Day effect. Use inventory and/or lead time buffers to absorb variation in customer demand.
7. Understand the information backbone that supports your value streams. Use business process kaizen to improve core processes. Engage planning and scheduling teams in improvement activity. Recognize that they are not the problem—they're the countermeasure.

(continued)

> *(continued)*
>
> 8. Provide information in small, frequent, digestible batches. Try to match information and production cycle times. Take information out of the box known as the computer and make it visible and understandable to users.
> 9. Understand and implement the Stabilize-Flow-Pull sequence in your supply chain.

STUDY QUESTIONS

1. Provide at least one example of the Nash Equilibrium:
   a. At work
   b. At home
2. Why does batch size determine cost structure? Provide at least three concrete examples from your organization.
3. Assess supplier connections in your organization. Are they direct, binary, and self-diagnostic? Explain your answer.
   a. How might you improve supplier connections?
4. Assess supplier pathways in your organization. Are they simple, prespecified, and self-diagnostic? Explain your answer.
   a. How might you improve supplier pathways?
5. Assess the stability of your current production and/or service schedules. Are you providing the Groundhog Day effect for your team members?
   a. If not, what are the sources of instability?
   b. How might you improve?
6. Define the three syllables that make up heijunka. Draw an image for each one.
7. Assess planning and scheduling processes in your organization.
   a. Are they standardized, visible, and shared?
   b. Are they capable?
   c. Are customer needs understood?
   d. How might you improve planning and scheduling processes in your organization?

Chapter 12 Dealers, Spielers, and Concealers

Fifteen hundred dealers remained in Taylor Motors' North American dealer network. They were angry and afraid. Just more than a year ago, we had sent sayonara letters to almost 1,800 of their colleagues; dealerships with low scores on customer satisfaction, sales effectiveness, profitability, and capitalization. We'd had no choice. Federal loans were contingent on an acceptable restructuring plan, and dealer rationalization was a big part of it.

Many dealers, still fearful of losing their franchises, had cut advertising spending, refused to order new vehicles, and concentrated on service and used vehicles. "We're doing everything to prepare in case we're not a Taylor Motors dealership a month from now," Bill Quigley told me during lunch at the Iron Horse.

Bill and his family owned the Quigley Family of Dealerships including 17 dealerships and 26 repair shops in New York, New Jersey, and Pennsylvania. I'd invited Bill to lunch to see if they'd be our pilot. Quigleys had been selling Taylor Motors' vehicles since the 1920s. Their support would go a long way.

Before the Chloe launch, I didn't know much about our dealers—only that they didn't feel like part of Taylor Motors. And, in fact, they weren't. Each dealer was a separate business entity, with its own objectives, plans, and incentives, which were often misaligned with ours. Yet to customers, our dealers *were* Taylor Motors. A shoddy dealership with poor layouts and cleanliness, shifty salespeople, and lousy customer service tarnished us almost as badly as a shoddy product.

Big as we were, Taylor Motors was just part of an ecosystem that included hundreds of parts suppliers upstream and hundreds of dealers downstream. We had to learn how to manage relationships that were simultaneously competitive and cooperative. The Four Rules were the means of managing this complexity; energy and creativity were the constraint.

Dealer margins had been eroding for a decade. The virtual marketplace had come between our dealers and customers. Net-based information and service brokers gave customers better information quicker. Independent auto superstores and distribution networks gave them better prices and service. Truth be told, the value proposition of Taylor Motors' dealers was weakening. We were losing our connection to the customer.

Elaine Miyazaki and Antonio Villarreal led Chloe's dealer-related activities. They proposed applying the recipe we were applying with our parts suppliers:

- Apply our core transformation process.
  - Executive development.
  - Lean coordinator network.
  - Focused activities through strategy deployment.
- Take a pilot approach.
  - Start with an influential family of dealerships, like Quigley.
- During the first six months, dealers keep all savings generated through kaizen. Savings thereafter would be split evenly.

Andy and I agreed. Bill Quigley liked the approach, especially getting help and keeping part of the savings. "We've had a terrible time, Tom. My bottom line is simple. You help my company save money and get better, I'm in."

"Glad to hear it," I told him. "So tell me, where does the shoe pinch?"

"We gotta sell more and spend less. It'd be good if Chloe's a hit, but Chloe's only one model. We need to get more people into our dealerships. We need to make more money on repair and maintenance. And we need to carry less stock and parts."

I shared Bill's objectives with Elaine, Antonio, and Andy. "The story's pretty clear," said Elaine. "Quigley's value proposition has been eroding. People don't like car salesmen or the lousy service they get at dealerships. If they could, many people would avoid the dealer entirely."

"So how do we sweeten the value proposition?" I asked.

"There has been much debate," said Antonio. "The consensus is dealerships have to get better at solving *all* the customer's mobility problems. It goes back to the question, *who are we?* I believe the correct answer is: *people who solve mobility problems.* The solution might be a new, used, or rental car, or it could be repair, maintenance, financing, or insurance. The solution might include pick-up services, kids play areas, easier return policies, and so on. Bottom line: Dealers have to reduce hassles."

Andy nodded. "Sales is the most important part of the Lean management system—because it is closest to the customer. Dealers have to learn to solve customer problems—a big change in thinking! Elaine-san, what is current thinking in the Taylor dealer network?"

"Mental models are like those we've seen across Taylor Motors, sensei," Elaine answered. "Dealers think in terms of silos: new and used car sales, parts, service, finance, human resources . . ."

"Dealers see the customer as an adversary," Antonio put in. "Someone you keep in the dark. So customers see car salesmen as hustlers who try to sell you what you don't want—at inflated prices."

"That's partly our fault," I commented. "We don't always give dealers the cars the customer wants."

"Production scheduling is a monster," Elaine said. "We need to apply heijunka *downstream* of the factory, too, in our distribution system."

"Let's take on that monster next year," I said. "It'll take years to tame."

"We must focus," Andy agreed.

"Any other mental models you want to highlight, Elaine?" I asked.

"Leaders are dictators," Elaine went on. "Not surprising—people who own dealerships are often big wheels in small communities. They're used to being top dog. Problems are garbage—keep them hidden. People are not to be trusted. Standards are complex, confusing, and developed on high . . ."

"So we should get a lot of traction with Lean basics," I offered.

Elaine nodded. "All the stuff we're applying across the Chloe platform applies in the dealer network."

"Lean *provision*[1] is the undiscovered country," said Antonio. "I've been learning about it. Here are the basic principles:

- Solve my problem completely by ensuring all goods and services work together.
- Don't waste my time.
- Provide exactly *what* I want.
- Provide it *when* I want it.
- Provide it *where* I want it.
- Minimize the number of decisions I need to make.

"Each question entails rich possibilities," he said. "Whoever, figures it out will earn a fortune . . ."

"Lean provision maps are a simple and effective way of making problems visible," Elaine added. "They're essentially value stream maps that illustrate the process from the customer and provider's point of view. Dealers will be shocked at how much they inconvenience their customers—and at how misaligned their provision processes are."

Elaine passed out a sample consumption/provision map for a typical car repair process—before and after application of Lean thinking. See Figures 12.1, 12.2, and 12.3.

The maps were simple and intuitive, and would prove to be a useful tool.

---

[1] *Lean Solutions*, by Dan Jones and James Womack, (Boston MA: Lean Enterprise Institute, 2005).

Car Repair **Before** Lean Processes

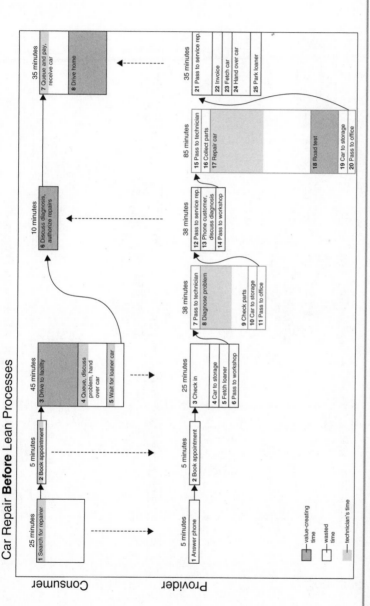

FIGURE 12.1 Harvard Business Review Car Repair Before Lean Processes

Source: "Lean Consumption," by Jim Womack and Dan Jones, *Harvard Business Review*, March 2005.

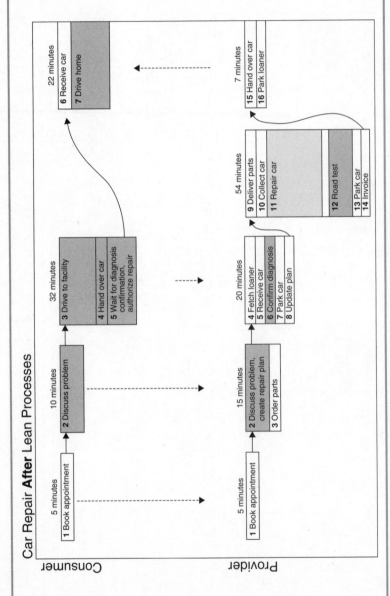

FIGURE 12.2 Harvard Business Review Car Repair After Lean Processes

Source: "Lean Consumption," by Jim Womack and Dan Jones, *Harvard Business Review*, March 2005.

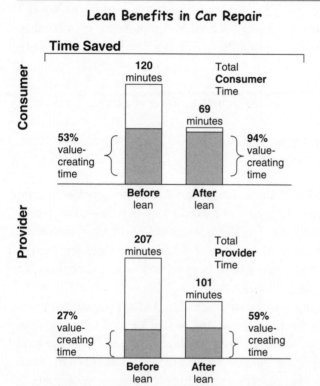

Lean Benefits in Car Repair

FIGURE 12.3   Harvard Business Review Lean Benefits in a Car Repair

Source: "Lean Consumption," by Jim Womack and Dan Jones, *Harvard Business Review*, March 2005.

Elaine and Antonio began by helping Bill Quigley implement strategy deployment in the Quigley dealership network. Quigley's hoshin was *Solve My Problem Completely,* in keeping with the first principle of Lean provision. The Quigleys' team developed and deployed mother A3 strategies in four focus areas: People, Customer Service, Delivery, and Cost. Bill chipped in by freeing up talented people to serve as Lean coordinators.

Elaine and Antonio held boot camps for executives and Lean coordinators. Over time, they helped build a lean coordinator network. Lean coordinators began to lead basic kaizen activity and to share what they'd learned. As with our suppliers, it would take years, but the benefits would be worth it.

How much more to tell you about our dealership work? We did some cool stuff. For example, we analyzed repair and maintenance demand at large dealerships and discovered a familiar pattern. Work comprised:

- Runners—High volume, less complex, lower cycle time work (e.g., routine repairs).
- Strangers—Low volume, more complex, lower cycle time work (e.g., unusual breakdowns).

We calculated Takt times, which gave us a sense of pace and rhythm, as in a car factory. It occurred to us that frontline people should be diagnosticians. The more we could glean from the initial chat with the customer, the better we could do triage and scheduling. We also implemented prediagnosis bays where we could confirm the nature of the work to be done.

Runner and stranger work were scheduled along predefined pathways (that is, predetermined routes and bays). We used big scheduling boards in each zone, which showed the day's work and ahead/behind status. We strengthened the process with visual management, standardized work, and replenishment pull for our most common parts. It took more than a year to get traction, but the savings were worth it. Bill Quigley became a Lean champion.

With Andy's help, we also began a pilot around advanced scheduling of repair and maintenance. Our model was the airline industry. Just as airline companies sell spaces on an airplane, Quigley's repair shops would sell slots in their schedule. The earlier the customer booked, the better the price. The idea was to lock in demand in advance so that we could apply the heijunka, or level loading concept. This would help us reduce repair lead times and cost, while improving productivity. The customer would get lower prices, less waiting, and better quality. It's a mind bender for Bill Quigley, but he agreed to run an experiment. Over time, we hope to develop a relationship with the customer—so we can solve his mobility problems completely.

Andy extended the concept to production. What if customers were able to preorder cars and other products—the way they preorder seats on an airplane? The earlier you order, the better price you get. The producer would get a more stable production schedule—the gold ring in manufacturing. The customer would get lower prices, quicker delivery, and better quality—a proverbial win-win.

Lean provision was a deep well of opportunity. We were barely rippling the surface. It would take years to fully harvest the potential. Being a Shusa was a long-term gig.

The Chloe launch was in the stretch run—less than two months to go! From design through to manufacturing, we had momentum and confidence. There was much to be discovered. We'd only made halting progress in our business processes. We'd barely explored the oceans known as supply chain and dealerships. Would Chloe have a soul, as Rachel had requested? The customer would decide. At the very least, we'd launch an excellent vehicle, on time and on budget.

Then Morgan and May struck again.

I could scarcely believe May's e-mail. "Given the importance of the Chloe launch, we feel an objective, third-party assessment would be beneficial. Chicago Consulting Group, one of the world's great consulting companies, has offered to provide this service for free. CCG has dispatched a team of Lean consultants who will audit various departments involved in the Chloe launch."

Rachel went directly to John Cafferty. Art Juna got wind of it and called Morgan on to the carpet. My irritation gave way to curiosity. What had triggered such a bizarre move? Chloe was in the stretch run and couldn't afford distractions. I'd asked Anne Smith to do some research on CCG. Their Lean practice was iffy. Lean is not amenable to the cookie-cutter approach that large consulting companies depend on. If Morgan felt we needed help, why would he wait until the last minute? Was J. Ed Morgan trying to wreck the Chloe launch? How could he possibly benefit?

Rachel and I quickly put together a game plan, which I laid out in a teleconference with Chloe platform leaders. Many of them were indignant. "What a dumb-ass move," said John Winter in his Alabama sing-song, "sending in green kids with sharp pencils . . ."

Our plan was to play nice while minimizing hassle. Chloe's overall approach and plan was sound; we were on track for our May 1 launch. Next day I got a call from Jack Spencer, head of CCG's Lean office. "Hi Tom, I wondered if I might visit your CMM offices to chat about the Chloe launch. I'd like to bring a couple of associates."

Like most large consulting companies in the post-crash world, CCG was anxious for business. CCG's business model appeared to be a broad pyramid—a handful of very smart people at the top, supported by hundreds of young MBAs, fresh out of Ivy League schools. I checked out their web site. Lean was just one of the arrows in their quiver, along with Six Sigma, Lean Six Sigma, and the like. Any port in a storm, I thought.

Jack Spencer had been a senior manager at Toyota Kentucky. Evidently, he didn't know Andy was working with us. I decided to have some fun. Spencer arrived later that week, two young MBAs in tow. No doubt they'd had high grade point averages. I remembered something Becky had said when I first interviewed her fresh out of engineering school. "I wasn't worried about my GPA. I was there to learn . . ."

"Welcome to CMM," I told them. "To be frank, we're not thrilled to have you here and won't be able to spend much time with you. Chloe is launching in less than two months. But we welcome any suggestions for improvement."

"I appreciate your candor, Tom," Spencer replied. A factory guy, uncomfortable in his suit, he seemed decent enough. Did he regret leaving Toyota?

"We've been building our Lean practice the past few years," he went on. "I've been through quite a few launches. Maybe we can offer some useful insights. I'd like to start with a tour of the gemba. That means the real place, where the real work gets done."

"Mary and Paul, our pilot area team leaders, will take you out," I told him.

Anne Taylor, my assistant at CMM, made a face after they'd left. "*Gemba, that means real place.* What a pin-head . . . and where'd they find those two automatons . . ."

"Now, now," I laughed. "They seem okay. In any event we'll be rid of them soon."

They came back an hour later. Jack Spencer was quiet. He didn't see what he expected to see. Andy had taken the CMM team under his wing. Our pilot area was as good as any at Toyota Kentucky. Spencer's associates had no idea what they were looking at. "Wow, your team really believes in their Lean program!" the young woman exclaimed.

"It's not a program," Anne said. "It's how we do business."

Then I gave them an overview of our upstream and downstream activities. Jack was pensive; the kids were writing down every word. Then there was a knock on the door. Andy Saito walked in.

"Konnichiwa, Jack-san. Long time no see."

Spencer sat bolt upright. "Saito-san, I had no idea . . ."

Andy bowed. "Tom-san and I have been working together."

"More than five years," I put in, "first at NJMM, now with the Chloe platform. Jack, you seem like a good guy, and I know you're just doing your job. But our philosophy is *learn-by-doing*. As I understand it, CCG's approach is to do it *for* the client. Capability versus dependency; that's a fundamental difference."

Jack shrugged. *I guess you're right.*

The meeting ended soon after. As we walked to the front entrance, we talked about Toyota's current problems and what it might do to recover. Spencer relaxed noticeably. "They need to get back to basics," he said, "and I think they will."

Spencer's associates peppered us with questions, scribbling furiously. Bright kids indeed. Would they get the mentorship they needed? Five years with a good sensei and they'd be all right. Jack could play that role—if he remained at CCG. Jack told us he'd joined them a year ago and had learned a great deal. I read between the lines. *Not sure CCG is for me . . .*

"If the Chloe launch is a dud," I joked, "Andy and I may start a consulting company."

Jack Spencer laughed. "I may be calling you."

The CCG audit petered out after a few more weeks. Their summary report essentially reinforced all the things we were working on. Their recommendations amounted to window dressing. Rachel replied politely: *thanks, but no thanks.* The episode was a blow to Morgan's credibility.

But the incident troubled me. Why was J. Ed Morgan trying to wreck the Chloe launch?

Process kaizen, Andy taught us, uncovers management system problems. Production scheduling was a monster system problem—one that we bumped up against repeatedly. But we couldn't touch it. Scheduling fell under Fred May's control. Neither he, nor his lieutenants, attended any boot camps. They resisted all our attempts at kaizen.

As long as May was around, we'd keep making the wrong stuff—and too much of it—frustrating our dealers, depleting our cash, and stressing our manufacturing plants and supply chain.

"Fred May keeps blocking scheduling system kaizen," I told Elaine.

We'd attended the daily pilot area report-out and were walking through assembly back to the obeya. Team members were cycling the new equipment. Bright winter sunshine came in through the high windows. It felt good to be in the factory.

"I think I may know why," Elaine said. "I've been analyzing our financial statements."

I raised my eyebrows. *Do tell* . . . Back in the obeya, Elaine went to a flip chart. "I need to give you some accounting basics first. Here's how information flows on financial statements." See Figure 12.4.

"Now let's compare two companies. One is a *mass* producer that builds in big batches and overproduces like crazy. The second is a *Lean* producer that builds in small batches to the customer order, and does *not* overproduce. Their sales, initial material costs, and labor costs are identical. What do the respective financial statements look like?"

Elaine passed out a spreadsheet. "What do you notice?" See Figure 12.5.[2]

Information Flow on Financial Statements

Profit & Loss Statement	Retained Earnings	Equity	Balance Sheet
Revenue			
- Cost of Goods Sold	Net Profit	Capital Stock	Net Profit
= Gross Profit	- Dividends	+ Retained Earnings	- Dividends
- Expenses	= **Retained Earnings**	= **Equity**	= **Retained Earnings**
= **Net Profit**	Reinvestment in the business		Reinvestment in the business

FIGURE 12.4   Information Flow on Financial Statements
Source: "Financial Aspects of Value Stream Transformation," by Sylvana LaSelva and Leslie Barker, Lean Pathways Fall Conference, Toronto, November 2009.

---

[2] I'm obliged to Leslie Barker and Sylvana LaSelva for these and other insights into the financial aspects of Lean. Many are based on their presentation, "Financial Aspects of Lean," Lean Pathways Spring Conference, Toronto, May 2009.

A Tale of Two Companies

Inventory and Profit		Mass Producer	Lean Producer
Beginning materials at cost		$ 5,000,000.00	$ 5,000,000.00
New purchases	+	$ 2,500,000.00	$ 1,250,000.00
Ending materials at cost	−	$ 5,000,000.00	$ 3,750,000.00
Material cost		$ 2,500,000.00	$ 2,500,000.00
Labor cost	+	$ 750,000.00	$ 750,000.00
Overhead cost	+	$ 1,000,000.00	$ 1,000,000.00
Actual costs		$ 4,250,000.00	$ 4,250,000.00
Deferred labor & overhead from inventory reduction	+	$0.00	$ 612,500.00
Cost of Goods Sold (COGS)		$ 4,250,000.00	$ 4,862,500.00
Income Statement			
Sales		$ 4,500,000.00	$ 4,500,000.00
COGS	−	$ 4,250,000.00	$ 4,862,500.00
Gross profit		*$ 250,000.00*	*−$ 362,500.00*
Cash Statement			
Purchase inventory		$ 2,500,000.00	$ 1,250,000.00
Labor costs	+	$ 750,000.00	$ 750,000.00
Overhead costs	+	$ 1,000,000.00	$ 1,000,000.00
Total cash used		*$ 4,250,000.00*	*$ 3,000,000.00*

Paying for the "sins of the fathers"

FIGURE 12.5 A Tale of Two Companies

Source: "Financial Aspects of Value Stream Transformation," by Sylvana LaSelva and Leslie Barker, Lean Pathways Fall Conference, Toronto, November 2009.

The income statement suggested the mass producer was profitable, and that the Lean producer was unprofitable. The cash statement told a different story. The mass producer's profitability was a mirage. It had sucked up far more cash supporting the same amount of sales. It was carrying twice as much inventory—and all the associated costs.

"The Lean company took an additional cost," I answered, "related to inventory reduction. It's based on the accounting principle called *matching*, and it seems wacky to me."

"You're not alone," said Elaine. "Standard costing is based on complex cost estimates and allocations. For example, when a product is *not* sold during a given reporting period, its costs plus margin are treated as an *asset*. An adjustment is made by moving the unused inventory plus costs onto the balance sheet. That *distorts* profitability. So Cost of Goods Sold is *lower* than it should be. It looks like we're making money—even when we aren't."

"Let me get this straight," I said. "Standard costing moves unsold inventory, plus related costs like labor, *from* the income statement *to* the balance sheet. And this makes things look better than they are."

Elaine nodded. "When we finally sell the excess inventory, we have to incur a cost called 'deferred labor and overhead from inventory reduction.' That's the so-called matching principle."

"That's nuts!" I exclaimed. "You're allowed to hide cost. It's a shell game. *Now you see it, now you don't.* I'm surprised it's legal." See Figure 12.6.

"It's legal," Elaine replied, "but not exactly kosher. Standard costing was developed for the mass production world. It's misleading in a Lean world. Sophisticated investors go to the cash statement, which gives a much more accurate picture."

I looked over Elaine's spreadsheet. "So that's why the Lean company incurs the extra $612,000 in cost. In effect, we're paying for the sins of the fathers."

Elaine nodded. "That's why I'm telling you about it. We have a ton of unsold Defiant inventory. If we have to pay for previous sins it'll look like Chloe's losing money."

I mulled it over. We were vulnerable. "I'll give Rachel a heads up. We'll need a plan . . ."

FIGURE 12.6   Standard Cost Shell Game

"Over time, we'd like to migrate to Lean accounting[3] and plain language financial statements," Elaine continued. "We want to use actual costs for each value stream with little or no allocation. We won't pretend inventory is an asset. We know it's the worst form of waste. To keep it under control, we'll let the customer pull it. We should be able to make better business decisions."

I shook my head. "Sounds good Elaine—but unlikely while Morgan and May are there."

"Funny you should mention them," Elaine said. "I've reviewed our financial statements going back 20 years. An interesting pattern is emerging . . ."

My brain began doing the rumba. "Let me guess . . . we've incurred false profits."

Elaine nodded. "And there's more. I have spies in Finance. Guess whose bonus has been tied almost exclusively to profitability?"

Now it was double-time rumba. "Morgan and May . . ."

---

[3] For a detailed discussion of Lean Accounting, the reader is referred to *Real Numbers*, by Jean Cunningham and Orest Fiume (Durhan, NC: Managing Times Press, 2003), and *Practical Lean Accounting*, by Brian Maskell and Bruce Baggaley (New York: Productivity Press, 2003).

I remembered all the end-of-quarter exhortations to "make the numbers," the desperate drive for more production, even when the market was soft. Then the catastrophic collapse of the past few years, as the house of cards came down. Had Morgan and May been profiting at the expense of the company?

"Elaine, we need to get this information to Rachel."

A week later, we did. Rachel thanked us and quoted Pink Floyd. "All in all, just another brick in the wall . . ."

Something was up.

Human resources (HR) was our other monster management system problem. HR had always seemed a black box, its processes and values opaque. Taylor Motors wasn't good at developing or motivating people. At NJMM, I'd found a process vacuum and had asked Antonio to develop a working HR system. It's all about people, Andy said.

Maude Beecher was no friend to the Chloe launch. She had ignored our requests to integrate the Lean coordinator position into broader career paths. She had supported Morgan's head count games, which hindered platform staffing. Moreover, like May, she jealously guarded her territory.

Under intense pressure from Rachel, Maude Beecher finally allowed us a brief, bizarre foray into human resources. Antonio led a three-hour introduction to Lean for Maude and her direct reports. Our plan was to

- Introduce the basics—Value and waste, standardized work, visual management, and core mental models.
- Do a gemba walk.
- Introduce the Big and Small process concept.

Then we break up into small groups and answer the core questions:

- Who is the customer?
- What do they value?
- What are the processes through which we provide value?

HR turned out to be an odd place. The HR team's consciousness of the customer, and of value and waste, were weak. Visual management was nonexistent. People insisted they had no problems. Everything is good, they told us, looking warily at Maude.

HR processes were invisible and vaguely defined. Objectives and strategies were also invisible. There was no ahead/behind consciousness. Much store was placed on *feelings*. "Tom, didn't you say *intuition* was just as important as data?" Maude asked, raising her eyebrows.

"Indeed I did," I responded.

"This place is weird," Elaine whispered during a break.

Antonio talked about the importance of management systems and drew out the People system we'd implemented at NJMM. Our purpose was to create value, he explained. We do this by understanding customers, and aligning our processes accordingly. Our People system is the most important system of all, Antonio went on. Lean is all about people.

Silence. I could hear the second hand on the wall clock. See Figure 12.7.

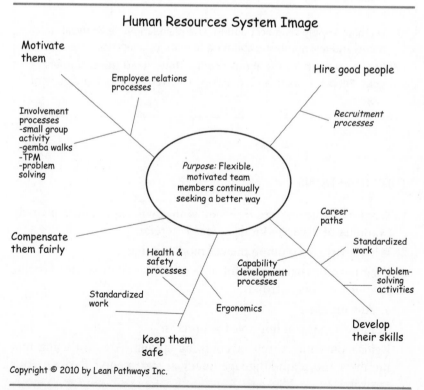

FIGURE 12.7   Human Resources System Image

Maude finally broke the silence. "Tom, you don't expect us to *do* this, do you?"

IMPLEMENTATION CHECKLIST

1. Understand and apply the principles of Lean provision in your retail operations.
2. Use Lean provision maps to better understand the customer's experience. Assess your corresponding provision processes and make countermeasures.
3. Make frontline people diagnosticians and, where possible, problem solvers.
4. Understand demand in your service work and define pathways for different value streams.
5. Recognize the difficulties posed by standard cost accounting and make necessary adjustments to ensure clarity and sound decision making.
6. Learn and apply Lean accounting. Use plain-language financial statements and real number accounting to make business decisions.
7. Recognize that Lean is about people. Understand the customers of your People system and develop a corresponding management system.

STUDY QUESTIONS

1. What is value in retail? From your own experience, provide examples of different kinds of waste in retail.
2. What are three common mental models in retail?
3. Do a Lean provision map for at least one retail or service process in your zone of control.
   a. Any insights?
   b. How might you improve the process?
4. Reflect on your current accounting system. Are you using real numbers and plain-language financial statements? Explain your answer.
   a. How might you improve your accounting system?

5. What is value in Human Resources? From your own experience, provide examples of different kinds of waste in HR.
6. What are three mental models common in HR?
7. What is the purpose of your organization's HR system?
8. What are the elements of your organization's HR system?
   a. What are its strengths and weaknesses?
   b. How might you improve your HR system?

Chapter 13   Scylla and Charybdis

It was the end of March and the snow was melting. We'd even had a few spring-like days, which reflected my frame of mind. My dad's health had stabilized. My ex-wife and I had mended our relationship and our kids were benefiting. Chloe was on track for her May 1 launch.

I'd also made up my mind to propose to Sarah. I wanted it to be special. Harry and I had been kicking around ideas. Harry had even bought a book, *The Utter Moron's Guide to Marriage Proposals*. That's the one for me, I told him.

But first I had to survive Chloe's report to the board of directors. We'd survived the slings and arrows of outrageous fortune—and of bozo finance executives. Now we had to make a good account before a newly activist board.

Before Art Juna became chairman, we had one of the least assertive boards in business. For years, critics carped that Taylor Motors needed directors with the chutzpah to force stodgy executives to ditch failed strategies and remake us into a twenty-first-century company. The Feds, in particular, wanted a hands-on board.

Now we had our most aggressive board ever, including several private equity guys. The board recently caused a stir by pushing back on a major investment in engine research. Though the board eventually supported the investment, management lost precious time building the business case. Some critics worried the board was overreaching. Our Chloe report wouldn't be business as usual.

Andy and I took the familiar 7:30 AM flight out of LaGuardia, Queens and Manhattan plunging below us. My jacket and tie felt strange. I'd never reported to the board before. I'd give it to them straight and let the pieces fall where they may. Chloe would be on time and on budget. She was a cool vehicle; though not a Prius-buster yet. Give us time, I thought. We'd addressed the customer's biggest issues; preliminary feedback was enthusiastic. Her new headlights, which made her look winsome, didn't hurt. It was the Seabiscuit effect—people were pulling for the underdog. I was confidant we'd hit our volume targets.

I looked across the aisle at Andy, who was snoozing, as he usually did on airplanes. Andy and Mrs. Yamamoto were spending more time together. They had just returned from a trip to Japan. Apparently, Mrs. Yamamoto and Andy's daughters, Yumi and Yamiko, had gotten along well. He seemed less lonely, less vulnerable. Maybe he was finally getting over Shizuko's death. Andy was spending less time with us now—a day or two per week. "You know what to do, Tom-san," he told me. "Not sure I do," I replied. I felt like a kid who'd found a few shiny stones at the edge of a vast ocean. The ocean beckoned but I didn't feel I was capable of navigating alone.

The plane began its descent into Detroit Metro Airport. I thought again of Detroit's decaying grandeur, the decrepitating fine homes and cracking boulevards, the muscle and magic, a distant memory. Could a phoenix rise out of these gray, slushy streets? Could Chloe be a small step toward that end?

We arrived at Taylor Motors' world headquarters an hour early so we could huddle with Rachel Armstrong and Bill Barrett. Security buzzed us through the glass doors. We took the elegant old elevator up to the executive offices. Brenda Davies was waiting and ushered us into Rachel's office. She and I swapped jokes as we walked through the plush hallways. She didn't call me McDuff-san, likely not wanting to confuse Andy.

Rachel and Bill Barrett were waiting for us. We exchanged greetings. Rachel invited us to sit at the conference table. "This'll be an unusual board meeting," she said. "At the end of it, Art Juna is going to make an announcement."

"Your report looks good, Tom," said Bill. "The board has been tracking Chloe's progress. Many board members have driven Chloe and are pleased with her. There shouldn't be any surprises. Art Juna is big fan."

"Art's been checking in with me, as you know," I said. "He seems like a tornado!"

"You got that right," Rachel laughed. "Saito-san, would you give us your perspective on the Chloe launch."

"Chloe activity is basically okay," Andy began. "Good progress in Design and Engineering. CMM factory is in good condition. Communication across the Chloe platform is much better. Thinking across the platform is beginning to change. There is much work to do in the supply chain and dealerships. Maybe two or three years. It is important to sustain Chloe module teams. They have learned to work together. We must not disrupt them through constant reorganization."

Andy passed out his personal Chloe dashboard, a two-sided 11- by 18-inch sheet, and did a zone by zone summary, starting with marketing and ending with dealers. Each chart included trend lines, Red/Green status, and a text box that told the story. It was vacuum-packed with insight.

Rachel and Bill absorbed Andy's report in silence. When Andy finished we discussed learning points and next steps. Rachel and Bill reiterated their commitment to the Shusa model and to our team. Go faster, they told us.

"Now we'd like to hear from you, Tom," Rachel said. "Any reflections, learning points, next steps?"

"Not sure where to start," I replied. "We have a bad case of Big Company Disease. We have smart, tenacious people. Most of them work in lousy processes, yet they keep going and somehow get stuff done. If we can eliminate process waste and hassle, we can challenge anybody. Doing so means involving everybody in problem solving.

"It also means applying the Four Rules to connect our silos, and the Four Capabilities to build our problem-solving capability. *See a problem, solve a problem, share what you've learned.* I've learned that complexity is a crude state. Simplicity marks the end of a process of refining. But simplicity is very hard and comes only after years of practice.

"I've also learned that business process kaizen is much harder than manufacturing kaizen. Waste upstream and downstream of manufacturing is usually invisible, processes and process ownership foggy, and mental models undeveloped. Kaizen has just begun to develop roots in our admin areas. Lean basics apply, but have to be translated."

"We need a yokoten plan, Tom," Bill Barrett said. "How will we share these lessons with other platforms?"

"Elaine Miyazaki has a plan," I answered. "And as you know, we have a playbook for each zone. Each playbook comprises simple one-pagers summarizing what we did, what worked, what didn't work and why. We call it our Book of Knowledge."

"Good start—we have years of work ahead of us," Rachel said. "Now I'd like to talk about today's board meeting. As Bill said, your presentation should go over well. You're on just before the break. *After* the break, Art Juna is making his announcement. There may be fireworks."

Puzzled, I looked over at Andy, who shrugged. "Anything you can share with us?" I asked.

Rachel shook her head. "Just keep your wits about you."

We walked down the hall past John Cafferty's office, and into the splendid boardroom. Antiques, rich paneling, Alfred Taylor's portrait, and the round mahogany table. The old boy looked good. If only you could talk, I thought.

Fresh coffee, fruit, and pastry were set out on elegant credenzas by the windows. Board members were chatting and taking in the panoramic view of the Detroit River. I saw as much dark hair as gray hair. Our board was younger than it had been in years.

There was John Cafferty chatting with J. Ed Morgan, May's hulking form looming nearby. Art Juna was chatting with an elegant red-haired woman. He acknowledged our presence with a nod. I knew so little about this world. Andy seemed centered and relaxed.

He raised a comical eyebrow. *Look at all these jokers.* I couldn't help smiling.

Art Juna called the meeting to order. He led us smartly through the agenda—minutes of the previous meeting, CEO's report, Finance Committee's report, and so on. I could tell he was following long-established etiquette.

Juna had an ex-marine's respect for time and structure. He insisted that board members come prepared and fully participate. Discussions were focused and meeting minutes concise. There would be no free riders.

Morgan had dominated Taylor Motors' board for almost two decades. Then Art Juna swept him aside. But Morgan didn't look beaten. He delivered the Finance Committee's report with effortless style. Morgan seemed confident and aloof. If Elaine's bonus analysis was right, he could afford to be.

Fred May glared at me, as usual. His body language was transparent: *I'll get you.* I resisted the temptation to blow him a kiss.

"Other business," Juna announced. "Tom Papas, chief engineer of the Chloe platform will provide a status update. Chloe is launching very soon. We're anxious to hear what you have to say, Tom. Then we'll take a 15-minute break."

My presentation went well. I described Chloe's overall objectives and plan and where we currently stood. I briefly described our overall approach and how it differed from previous launches. I showed photos of improvement activities and talked about Big Company Disease and the importance of yokoten in Design. I gave a brief tribute to Andy Saito and thanked Rachel for her support.

"Japanese words and Japanese systems . . ." J. Ed Morgan said, sounding like the Prince of Wales. "My question is . . . how well do these apply at Taylor Motors? We have rich history and culture of our own. Why copy?"

Very smooth, I thought. Reframing the question—us versus them—and sowing doubt thereby. He didn't want to talk specifics, where Chloe was solid.

"We've had good success with Lean at our companies," said one of the private equity guys. "It's just good business."

"With great respect to our *new* board member," Morgan replied, "the automotive business is unlike any business in *your* portfolio."

Morgan had effectively marshaled his allies. The debate bounced back and forth as in a tennis match, but on a court Morgan had defined. I marveled at his skill and realized we were vulnerable. As Elaine had demonstrated, Morgan could use standard costing to make Chloe look like a failure. In particular, I remembered a Fred May boast. *I can make the financial statements say anything I want them to say.*

Juna watched Morgan the way a mongoose watches a cobra. After a few more minutes, he brought the discussion to a close. The agenda minutes would record the Morgan faction's reservations and our allies' rebuttals. We'll have a 15-minute break, Juna announced.

I walked to the credenzas by the window and poured myself a coffee. It was a typical Michigan winter day. The Detroit River mirrored the steel gray sky. Rachel came over. Well done, she said. Bill patted me on the back. Over by the Taylor portrait, Andy and Art Juna were having an animated chat.

I finished my coffee and took a walk to stretch my legs. As I passed Morgan's office I heard a voice call out, "Hey Papas, I want to talk to you."

It was Fred May. I walked into Morgan's office. It was even grander than Rachel's. "Anything I can do for you, Fred?"

"One of your people has been snooping around," said May, walking toward me. "Ms. *Miyazaki* has been asking questions about bonus payments. I don't like that."

"Have you got a problem with Elaine's name?" He was backing me into a corner. The May Treatment.

"Not at all," he said, crowding in on me, "but you're going to have a big problem if Ms. Miyazaki goes any further."

I remembered Rachel's admonition. *Keep your wits about you.* But I was sick of the bastard. "Fred, you talk big. But I'll bet you're *soft* inside, soft as *slime* . . ."

May grabbed my collar. With his other hand, he tried to pin my throat to the wall. Everything slowed down. I was back in the dojo at New York Aikikai. As in a dream, I put a hand in May's face and stepped to my left, drawing him off balance. I turned his wrist over—and bowed *slowly*. I didn't want to hurt him.

FIGURE 13.1   The May Treatment

Ryokatatatori-nikkyo. May began to feel the pain; his face turned red with panic.

I eased the pressure on May's wrist. "Next time, I'll put you through the floor." See Figure 13.1.

I heard Brenda's sing-song voice. "Now, now, boys, mustn't do anything to scare the horses."

I released May's arm. "Good timing, Mactavish. Shall we go?"

We walked out of Morgan's office and back to the boardroom. May didn't follow us and didn't return to the meeting. The world sped back up. In fact, my heart was racing.

"Sonofabitch attacked me," I said, the realization setting in.

"He got more than he bargained for," said Brenda, pouring me an orange juice. "Glad I followed you."

Rachel came over. "Everything all right?"

I nodded. "Just had an altercation with May. Brenda extracted me."

Art Juna called the meeting to order and worked through Other Business, Old and New. The last agenda item was Announcements.

"I have important news, which must remain confidential," Art Juna began. "Federal authorities have been investigating a member of our board—and have found serious irregularities."

The room became very quiet. Art looked directly at J. Ed Morgan. "In fact, charges are imminent and will be announced in the next few days. Our stock may get hammered but should recover once the full story gets out. Again, please keep this confidential."

Morgan had turned white as a ghost. The meeting was adjourned.

The story broke a few days later. J. Ed Morgan and members of Scylla Capital Management were indicted on 24 counts of racketeering, conspiracy to commit fraud, and a series of lesser offenses. They were accused of deliberately conspiring to devalue Taylor Motors for personal benefit in preparation for a takeover bid by Scylla. Morgan's lawyers claimed their client was innocent of all charges and this was another example of the government's witch hunt against private industry.

Morgan was allegedly in line for a huge payoff and a senior executive position in the new order. Scylla would pick up a big stake in Taylor Motors for a song. The past few years began to make sense. Morgan's opposition to all our improvement efforts, all the harassment. I wondered about May's role. Sure enough, he was indicted a few days after Morgan.

Soon after, I was sitting in the Humpty Dumpty watching CNN with Dad and Uncle Angie. The business report came on and I got to see Morgan and May do the perp walk yet again. "Do you know those two bums?" Uncle Angie asked.

I nodded. "They've caused me a lot of trouble."

"LOUSY CROOKS!" said my dad. "PFFT, I SPIT IN THEIR GENERAL DIRECTION!" He was feeling better.

"Our company has survived Scylla and Charybdis," I said.

"What are they, car makes?" asked Angie.

"No, sea monsters from Greek mythology," I replied. "They lie on either side of a narrow strait. Scylla is a six-headed creature who eats sailors that get too close. Charybdis is a gigantic whirlpool that sucks vessels down and crushes them. Last year we were almost sucked down by an economic whirlpool. And now we've survived a predatory private equity firm. Hopefully, the worst is over for us."

Dad looked at Angie. "Tommy's been working very hard lately. Maybe a bit too hard. . . ."

STUDY QUESTIONS

1. Tom suggests the remedy to Big Company Disease: See a problem, solve a problem, share what you've learned.
   a. Draw it out[1] using images and examples from your personal experience.
   b. Do you agree with Tom's remedy? Explain why or why not.
   c. What additional steps would you take to treat Big Company Disease?
2. "Complexity is a crude state," Tom says. "Simplicity marks the end of a process of refinement."
   a. Do you agree or disagree? Explain your thinking.
   b. Give at least three examples of this principle from your experience.
3. What are three things you learned reading this book. Draw them out.
4. Describe three ways you will apply the lessons learned in this book.

---

[1] *The Back of the Napkin*, by Dan Roam (New York: Penguin, 2008), illustrates the power of visual thinking and provides tips on how to get started.

Chapter 14 Be My Phenomena

April rains washed out the grimy slush of winter. Central Park sprouted greenery. Cherry trees bloomed in the Brooklyn Botanical Garden. Sarah, the girls, and I took in the Easter parade. Sarah was Catholic and that night we attended Easter Mass at St. Patrick's Cathedral. A week later we celebrated Greek Easter at St. Irene's in Astoria. Then we had a feast at Uncle Louie's. Mama made baklava and spanakopita. My aunts chipped in with other delicacies. The girls ran wild with their cousins.

Meanwhile, Harry and I were noodling proposal ideas. Given Chloe's imminent launch, I let my brother take the lead. I wanted to do something special for Sarah, something she'd remember. I expected her to accept my proposal, although I wasn't positive. One more thing to worry about.

The Park is an art deco treasure, a grand hotel in the old style. I love the mosaic floors and the four-sided clock in the main lobby. I love the antique elevators that take you to the Top of the Park, my favorite rooftop bar. The outdoor patio is magic on a balmy night.

Gus Lambrakis, the head bartender, is an old buddy of Dad's. He has great stories about the movie stars, mobsters, and mental cases he's served over the years. "John Wayne . . . of the old-time stars, he was my favorite. What a gentleman! Nowadays, I'd say Tom Hanks. Tom is good boy. He is like us. He married a Greek girl, you know . . ."

Gus's son, Paul, is headwaiter. I talked to them both in advance, explaining what was up and what I needed them to do. "Wonderful news, my boy!" said Gus.

"She hasn't accepted yet."

"Don't worry, she will," said Paul. "We'll make it extra special."

"Just don't go overboard, okay? Sarah likes things understated. We need subtlety and finesse . . . ."

Paul gave me a thumbs up. "Subtlety and finesse. You can count on me!"

Sarah and I would sit at our favorite table. I'd give Paul the engagement ring and he'd put our plan into action. "And please don't tell anyone. I'd like it to be intimate."

Paul brought a forefinger to his lips. "Sealed, Tommy, these lips are sealed!"

I watched the weather reports closely. We needed a warm evening. Finally, the third week of April, we got one. The window of opportunity was narrow though. Paul was leaving around midnight. He had an early-morning flight to Greece and would be gone for three weeks. With that and the Chloe launch, I might have to defer my plans for a month.

It was Saturday night and we'd invited our friends, Joe and Tania Grace, to our apartment for dinner. Joe is acting plant manager at NJMM. I'm pushing to make the position permanent. Tania taught grade school but now stays home with their three kids.

Sarah and I served meze, Greek salad, and lamb souvlaki. We also served Greek wine, a white moschofilero, and a red mavrodafni. Greek varietals are making a splash on the international scene.

Dinner was fun. I kept my eye on the clock. We should be okay, I thought. Joe and Tania usually leave at around 10:00 PM. That'll give us time to catch a cab into the city.

"Nice to be without the kids," said Joe, squeezing Tania's hand.

"Guess we're lucky," I said. "We have every other weekend free."

Tania smiled. "Enjoy it."

We chatted for a while. Joe and Tania were relaxed and seemed in no hurry. Ten o'clock came and went. I began to worry. What if they stayed late? I decided to nudge things along.

"This wine's getting to me," I said, stifling a yawn. "I feel dopey . . ."

"You were fine a few minutes ago," said Sarah. "Are you okay?"

"Just a bit tired. Sneaks up on you, I guess . . ."

Pretty soon everyone was yawning. We walked Joe and Tania to the elevator. I'd call them the next day to explain, and hopefully to share some good news.

"Does sneak up on you," said Sarah. "I'm ready for bed."

"I've got my second wind," I told her. How about a nightcap?

"Are you sure? You were falling asleep. . . ."

"Strange, eh? Must be the Chloe launch. Anyhow, it's a beautiful night. How about the Top of the Park?"

A taxi took us through the Lincoln Tunnel and into the city. Step on it, I'd whispered to the cabbie. It was 11:30 PM when we got to the hotel. Paul was leaving in 30 minutes. We took the elevator up to the rooftop bar.

Paul saw us walk in and hurried over. "Tom, Sarah, so good to see you. We have a table for you."

"That's strange," said Sarah. "How'd you know we were coming?"

"Ah, just a wild guess," Paul stammered. "It's a nice night. Ah, Tom and Sarah often come here. Who knows, maybe they'll come tonight. . . ."

Paul led us to a table overlooking Central Park, and framed by Manhattan's speckled canyons. He gave me a not-so-subtle wink. I tried not to notice.

"Paul's acting strange," said Sarah. "Is he okay?"

"He's going to Greece tomorrow morning," I offered. "Maybe he's already in holiday mode."

Paul returned to take our order. Sarah went with her favorite, the green apple martini. I ordered a bloody caesar. After a moment, I excused myself. I found Paul and pulled him behind a column.

"No need to keep winking. Remember, subtlety and finesse."

"Subtlety and finesse," Paul repeated. "Got you, Tom!"

I reached into my pocket. "Here's the ring. Drop it into the *green* drink—not the red one. Got it? The *green* drink. . . ."

"The green drink," said Paul, like someone under hypnosis.

I took a deep breath and returned to our table.

"What were you doing behind that column?" Sarah asked.

"Asking Paul about his trip," I said brightly. "He's a lucky guy. Wish we were going . . ."

Sarah gave me a puzzled look. I looked across the patio and into the bar. A dozen people or so sat grinning and waving at the grand window. A guy gave me a thumbs up. Another guy gave me an over-the-head handshake, like a wrestling champion. I put two and two together. Paul was singing like a canary. Everybody in the bar knew what was up.

Paul came out with our drinks. "The *green* drink for the lady," he said, looking at me significantly.

Sarah took a sip of her martini. "It's perfect. . . . Thanks, Paul."

Paul gave me a covert A-okay and headed back into the bar. I took a long pull on my a bloody caeser. Three ounces of vodka, celery sticks, horseradish . . . I calmed down.

We touched glasses. Then I realized, *I can't see the engagement ring*. Did Paul forget? *No! Sarah's drink is opaque.* . . .

I began to worry. What if she chokes? What if she swallows it? What if she *spits it out*? It'll fall 20 stories to Park Avenue.

"You know, Sarah," I said, "a martini should be *savored*. Small sips, that's what I always say."

Sarah rolled her eyes. We sat there, enjoying the view, spied upon by half the bar, and me ready to do the Heimlich maneuver. See Figure 14.1.

"Wait a minute, hold on. . . ." said Sarah, pulling something out of her mouth. "There's something in my drink. It's somebody's *ring*. . . ."

"Who do you think it belongs to?"

"I don't know, the waiter, the bartender . . . ?"

"Take a guess," I said.

Sarah looked at the ring—and at me. Her eyes welled up. "You're a nut . . ."

Tom's Proposal

Copyright © 2010 by Lean Pathways Inc.

FIGURE 14.1   Tom's Proposal

"And you, my dear, are a phenomena. The question is, will you be *my* phenomena?"

Sarah nodded. You can imagine the rest. People poured onto the patio. Gus came out with a bottle of champagne. On the house, he said.

"Didn't I tell you?" Paul crowed. "Everything worked out great!"

Chloe's launch was a partial success. We met our May 1 launch date and ramp-up schedule. Prelaunch orders and reviews were positive and suggested we'd easily meet our volume targets. We also met our quality and cost targets.

Our silos were more focused and better aligned. Handoffs were better, problems more visible, and countermeasures quicker. Our boot camps had grounded our executives in the fundamentals. Our Lean Coordinator Network numbered almost a hundred. These young leaders had led well over a hundred kaizen workshops. Lean thinking had developed tentative roots outside of manufacturing.

But the roots were shallow. And we'd barely scratched the surface in our supply chain and dealer network. Had our thinking really changed? Had we internalized the fundamentals? It had taken a near-death experience to open the door. Would we walk through it, now that the crisis was receding?

We'd lived to fight another day—that's all.

John Cafferty resigned soon after. Art Juna made the announcement at a hastily convened press conference, saying the board determined the company wasn't changing quickly enough. Art Juna would serve as interim CEO, and an international search for a new CEO was planned. Art thanked Cafferty for his work during a period of challenge and change, but said it is time to accelerate the pace of rebuilding Taylor Motors.

J. Ed Morgan, Fred May, and their Scylla co-conspirators are in court facing racketeering, and a host of lesser charges. Pundits expect Morgan and May to plead guilty to the latter, in return for the Feds dropping the former. They'll likely face massive fines and several years in prison.

"What motivates a man like Morgan?" I asked.

Sarah and I were having a drink on our balcony. Tugboats were churning along the Hudson River. The sun had set. The sky was purple with yellow and orange streaks.

"Hard to say," said Sarah. "Is it money? I imagine he has more than he could spend. Power? He had plenty of that, too."

Stars began to come out, one after another. There was Venus.

"What motivates a man like Andy Saito?" Sarah asked.

"Ethics," I replied. "The desire to do the right thing. I've been thinking about the cardinal virtues: Temperance, Prudence, Courage, and Justice.[1] I learned them in Sunday school. I've relearned them working with Andy."

"How do you mean?"

"The cardinal virtues inform the Plan-Do-Check-Adjust cycle, our expression of the scientific method. They also provide constancy of purpose. Andy taught us the water ring model of leadership. Just as water rings emanate outward when a pebble drops into a stream, everything a leader does is magnified.

"People won't follow a swine, at least not willingly. That's what people like Morgan and May don't understand. You can't hold power through fear—only through love."

---

[1] Readers interested in virtue ethics are directed to the splendid *A Short Treatise on the Great Virtues*, by Andre Comte-Sponville (New York: Henry Holt, 1996).

"Good lord, is this a factory manager talking?"

I smiled. "Must be the vino. Anyhow, of all the cardinal virtues, I find Temperance the most difficult, especially with us getting married and maybe having kids. My mentor paid a heavy price for his *intemperance*. I don't want to make the same mistake."

"Glad you're aware of it. I *love* your energy. Your challenge is to harness it, so it doesn't control you."

"You'll help me, I trust?"

She smiled, nodded. "Your relationship with Andy reminds me of an old fairy tale—*Iron John*. Want to hear it?"

A king sends a huntsman into the forest—he never returns. The king sends more, each meeting the same fate. The king proclaims the woods as dangerous and off-limits to all.

A hunter hears of this perilous forest and asks permission to enter it, so he can discover the fate of the others. He is allowed to enter with his dog. They come to a lake in the middle of the forest, and the dog is dragged underwater by a giant hairy arm.

Next day, the hunter returns with a group of men to empty the lake. They find a naked man with skinlike iron and long shaggy hair all over his body. They put him in chains and bring him back to the castle. He is locked in a courtyard cage and kept as a curiosity. No one is allowed to set the wild man free, on penalty of death.

Not long after, the young prince is playing with a ball in the courtyard. The ball rolls into the cage and the wild man picks it up. "I'll only return it if you set me free," he tells the prince. "The only key to the cage is hidden under the queen's pillow."

Although he's afraid, the prince sneaks into his mother's room and steals the key. He releases the wild man, who tells him his name is Iron John. The prince fears he will be punished for setting the wild man free. Iron John agrees to take the prince with him into the forest.

Iron John turns out to be a powerful being who guards many treasures. He asks the prince to watch over his well, but warns him not to let anything touch it because it will turn instantly to gold. The prince obeys at first, but begins to play in the well, finally turning all his hair into gold. Disappointed, Iron John sends the boy away to experience poverty and struggle. "If you ever need anything," he tells the prince, "call out my name three times."

The prince travels to a distant land and offers his services to its king. Because he is ashamed of his golden hair, the prince refuses to remove his cap before the king. He is sent to assist the gardener.

When war comes to the kingdom, the prince sees a chance to make a name for himself. He calls upon Iron John who gives him a horse, armor, and a legion of warriors to fight with him. The prince successfully defends his new homeland, but returns all that he borrowed to Iron John before returning to his former position.

In celebration, the king announces a banquet and offers his daughter's hand in marriage to any one of the knights who can catch a golden apple that will be thrown into their midst. The king hopes that the mysterious knight who saved the kingdom will show himself.

Again the prince asks Iron John for help, and again Iron John disguises the prince as the mysterious knight. Though the prince catches the golden apple and escapes, and does so again on two more occasions, he is eventually found out. The prince is returned to his proper station and claims the princess' hand in marriage.

As they're sitting at the marriage feast, the music suddenly stops, the doors open and a splendid king enters with his retinue. He goes up to the prince, and embraces him. "I am Iron John, and was by enchantment a wild man. But you have set me free. All the treasures I possess shall be your property."

I liked the story. "There's a lot in there. I'll have to think about it."

"It's a magic story," Sarah replied. "It helped inspire the men's movement."

"Really? I didn't think it was *that* good."

Sophie and Helen were understandably ambivalent about Daddy getting married again. Like all kids, they wanted mommy and daddy to live together. I encouraged them to bring all their questions and concerns to the surface.

"Your mommy and daddy love you more than anything in the world," I told them. "We got married because we really wanted to have you. But we didn't get along, and we're happier living apart."

"Is Sarah going to be our mommy?" Helen asked.

"No, Helen. Nobody will ever replace your mommy."

"Will we still spend time with you?"

"Of course you will. In fact, mommy wants us to spend even more time together."

"Do you love Sarah more than us?" Sophie asked.

"No, Sophie. I love you and Helen more than anyone in the whole world."

"Then, I guess it's okay if you get married," said Sophie.

Sarah and I were married that summer at St. Irene's. We had our reception at the Boy on a Dolphin banquet hall by the East River. Our families' combustible mix—Greeks and Hungarians—concerned me. "It's like mixing matter and antimatter," I told Harry. "How do we avoid fights?"

"Impossible!" Harry laughed. "Let's ask them to hold off till Father Karras goes home."

Sarah was radiant in her grandmother's wedding dress. Harry was best man. Sophie and Helen were charming flower girls. My folks sat with Sarah's parents and got along well with them. Mama kept thanking St. Spyridon. Dad complained about the food. There were no fights.

Harry and Uncle Angie did the Suckling Pig dance, wearing chef's hats and aprons, and brandishing long knives. They danced around the head table asking for bids on the suckling pig. Tens, twenties, and even fifty-dollar bills started to fly. Uncle Louie discreetly swept up the proceeds.

Andy sat near the head table with Mrs. Yamamoto, a lively woman with a round, happy face. Her deceased husband had also been an executive with a Japanese transplant company. Andy was trying to explain the mayhem. They seemed a good fit. "So nice to meet you, Tom-san," she'd said, shaking my hand vigorously. Andy had bowed. "Omedetou goziamasu." *Congratulations.*

"Arigato gozaimashita," I'd replied. *Thanks for all you've done for me.*

After dinner we pushed back the tables. Uncle Angie and the band took their places. Angie pointed his clarinet to the ceiling and let loose an amorous donkey wail. The band joined in. It was a *Kalamatiano*, the most popular Greek dance of all. Sarah and I led the dancers. Everybody joined in—old, young, skinny, fat, elegant, and awkward. Andy and Mrs. Yamamoto squeezed in beside Mama and Dad. And so it went the whole splendid evening.

The Dance

Copyright © 2010 by Lean Pathways Inc.

FIGURE 14.2   The Dance

During the bouquet toss, I slipped out onto the balcony—and found Andy there. I asked the bartender for two glasses of Japanese plum wine. We raised our glasses. *Yiamas.*

I looked across the East River. Another indigo night. Manhattan seemed a glittering chessboard, the famous buildings, speckled chess pieces. Five years earlier I'd stood on this same spot and felt my life turning around. I'd come full circle.

I told Andy about Iron John. He grinned. "Old Japanese story."

Of course. . . .

"You've enriched me," I told him. "I am in your debt, sensei."

"It was my pleasure. You are a sensei now."

"I feel like a clown," I said. "You're not going to disappear, are you?"

"I would like to drop in from time to time."

"That would be good."

The music was starting up again. We went inside to join the dance. See Figure 14.2.

STUDY QUESTIONS

1. Define *ethics*. Draw out your thoughts.
   a. Why is the study of ethics important, especially for leaders?
2. What is Temperance? Draw it out.
   a. How does Temperance relate to the PDCA cycle?
3. What is Prudence? Draw it out.
   a. How does Prudence relate to the PDCA cycle?
4. What is Courage? Draw it out.
   a. How does Courage relate to the PDCA cycle?
5. What is Justice? Draw it out.
   a. How does Justice relate to the PDCA cycle?

Glossary

4 Ms: Man/woman, machine, method, and material.

affinity diagram: A tool for gathering and grouping ideas; one of the new seven quality tools; used in hoshin planning.

aikido: A Japanese martial art founded by Morehei Ueshiba.

andon: A line stop; typically a cord that a worker can pull to stop the assembly line when he or she detects a defect; an example of jidoka.

asaichi: "Morning market" in Japanese; a quality activity that entails reviewing the previous day's most important defects and doing on-the-spot problem solving.

batch production: The practice of making large batches of a particular item so as to realize (supposed) efficiencies of equipment, materials, and map-power.

cell: An arrangement of people, machines, materials, and methods such that processing steps are adjacent and in sequential order so that parts can be processed one at a time (or in some cases in a consistent small batch that is maintained through the process sequence). The purpose of a cell is to achieve and maintain efficient continuous flow.

change over time: The time it takes for a piece of equipment to change over from one product to another; usually measured from the last good previous part or service to the first subsequent good part or service.

continuous flow: In its purest form continuous flow means that items are processed and moved directly to the next process one piece at a time. Each processing step completes its work just before the next process needs the item, and the transfer batch size is one. Also known as one-piece flow and "make one, move one."

cycle time: The actual time is takes to complete a process from start to finish to produce one unit (of product or service).

deshi: Student.

dojo: Training hall.

5 S: A system of workplace standardization and organization. The five Ss are sort, set in order, shine, standardize, and sustain.

Five Why analysis: Method of root cause analysis that entails asking why continually until the root cause(s) of a problem is uncovered.

flow: See continuous flow.

Four capabilities: Four capabilities of operationally outstanding organizations; the capabilities deal with Standards, Problem Solving, Shared Learning, and Role of the Leader.

Four Rules: Four organizing principles that underlie the Lean management system; the rules deal with Standard, Connections, Pathways, and Improvement.

gemba: The real place or the specific place. Usually means the shop floor and other areas where work is done.

genchi genbutsu: Go see; go to the real place and see what is actually happening.

GTS: Grasp the situation; the heart of PDCA.

heijunka: Production leveling; leveling the demand signal by volume and mix so as to protect the producer from excessive variation; literally, Level + Production Ratios + Continuous Improvement.

hoshin kanri: A strategic planning system developed in Japan and North America over the past 30 years. Also known as strategic policy deployment. Metaphorical meanings include "ship in a storm going in the right direction" and "shining needle or compass."

hoshin planning: See strategy deployment.

jidoka: Automation with a human mind. Developing processes with both high capability (few defects made) and containment (defects contained in the zone).

jishuken: An autonomous study group seeking improvement in a core business need; fresh eyes.

just-in-time: Providing the right part or service, at the right time, in the right quantity; the elements of JIT are Takt, Flow, and Pull.

kaikaku: A breakthrough improvement.

kaizen: Continuous incremental improvement. Kaizen activity should involve everyone regardless of position.

kanban: A small sign or signboard, an instruction to produce or supply something; usually a card; usually includes supplier and customer names, and information on transportation and storage; a central element of the just-in-time system. There are two types of production and withdrawal kanbans.

management by objectives: The precursor to hoshin planning; introduced by Peter Drucker in his 1954 book, *The Practice of Management*.

muda: Waste; there are 7 + 1 wastes: motion, conveyance, defects, overprocessing, waiting, inventory, overproduction, and knowledge.

mura: Unevenness, variation.

muri: Hard to do, strain, overburden.

nemawashi: Literally means "to prepare a tree for transplanting"; refers to the formal and informal method of gaining consensus prior to the implementation of a hoshin or plan.

PDCA: The plan, do, check, adjust cycle developed by Walter Shewhart in the 1930s and refined by W. Edwards Deming.

pokayoke: Defect-proofing; an inexpensive robust device that eliminates the possibility of a defect by alerting the operator that an error has occurred.

pull: To produce an item only when the customer asks for it. Typically, the customer "withdraws" the item and we "plug the gap" created thereby.

push: To produce an item irrespective of actual demand; creates the muda of overproduction.

SMART: Simple, Measurable, Achievable, Reasonable, and Trackable. Refers to goals and targets.

sensei: Teacher; one who has gone before.

Shusa: A leader with total responsibility for the development and success of a product line; also known as Chief Engineer.

store: A controlled inventory of items that is used to schedule production at an upstream process. Usually located near the upstream process to make customer requirements visible. Also called a supermarket.

strategy deployment: A strategic planning system developed in Japan and North America over the past 30 years.

supermarket: See store.

Takt: Available production time divided by demand; the pace of production synchronized with the rate of sales.

tree diagram: A tool used for mapping tasks for implementations; used in hoshin planning.

total productive maintenance (TPM): An integrated set of activities aimed at maximizing equipment effectiveness by involving everyone in all departments at all levels, typically through small group activities; TPM entails implementing the 5 S system, measuring the six big losses, prioritizing problems, and applying problem solving with the goal of achieving zero breakdowns.

value stream map: A Lean technique used to analyze the flow of materials and information required to bring a product or service to a consumer. At Toyota, where the technique originated, it is known as "material and information flow mapping."

yokoten: Shared, experiential learning across an organization.

References

I have found the books below particularly helpful in understanding the Lean system.

Balle, Michael, and Freddie Balle. *The Gold Mine*. Cambridge, MA: Lean Enterprise Institute, 2005.

Baudin, Michel. *Lean Logistics*. New York: Productivity Press, 2004.

Dennis, Pascal. *Andy & Me: Crisis and Transformation on the Lean Journey*. New York: Productivity Press, 2005.

Dennis, Pascal. *Lean Production Simplified: A Plain Language Guide to the World's Most Powerful Production System*. New York: Productivity Press, 2007.

Dennis, Pascal. *Getting the Right Things Done: A Leader's Guide to Planning and Execution*. Cambridge, MA: Lean Enterprise Institute, 2006.

Galsworth, Gwen. *Visual Systems: Harnessing the Power of a Visual Workplace*. New York: AMACOM, 1997.

Grief, Michel. *The Visual Factory: Building Participation Through Shared Information*. Portland, OR: Productivity Press, 1991.

Hopp, Wallace, and Mark Spearman. *Factory Physics*. New York: McGraw-Hill, 2000.

Jarvis, Jeff. *What Would Google Do?* New York: Harper Luxe, 2009.

Jones, Daniel, and James Womack. *Lean Solutions: How Companies and Customers Can Create Value and Wealth Together*. New York: Simon & Schuster, 2005.

Jones, Daniel, and James Womack. *Lean Thinking: Banish Waste and Create Wealth in Your Corporation*. New York: Simon & Schuster, 1996.

Liker, Jeffrey. *The Toyota Way*. New York: McGraw-Hill, 2004.

Liker, Jeffrey, and David Meier. *The Toyota Way Field Book*. McGraw-Hill, 2006.

Liker, Jeffrey, and James Morgan. *The Toyota Product Development System*. New York: Productivity Press, 2006.

Monden, Yasuhiro. *Toyota Production System: An Integrated Approach to Just-in-Time*, 2nd ed. Norcross, GA: EMP, 1993.

Ohno, Taiichi. *Toyota Production System: Beyond Large-Scale Production*. Portland, OR: Productivity Press, 1988.

Reinertsen, Donald. *Managing the Design Factory*. New York: Free Press, 1997.

Roam, Dan. *The Back of the Napkin*. New York: Penguin Group, 2008.

Rother, Mike, and John Shook. *Learning to See: Value Stream Mapping to Add Value and Eliminate Muda*. Cambridge, MA: Lean Enterprise Institute, 1999.

Shook, John. *Managing to Learn*. Cambridge, MA: Lean Enterprise Institute, 2006.

Spear, Steven. *Chasing the Rabbit*. New York: McGraw-Hill, 2009.

Suzaki, Kiyoshi. *The New Shop Floor Management*. New York: Free Press, 1993.

Toyota Motor Corporation. *The Toyota Production System*. Operations Management Consulting Division and International Public Affairs Division. Toyota City: Toyota Motor Corporation, 1995.

Ward, Allen. *Lean Product and Process Development*. Cambridge, MA: Lean Enterprise Institute, 2007.